47x 8/13√12/14

Baby Laughs

Also by Jenny McCarthy

Belly Laughs:
The Naked Truth About Pregnancy and Childbirth

Baby Laughs

The Naked Truth About the
First Year of Mommyhood

Jenny McCarthy

DUTTON

DUTTON
Published by Penguin Group (USA) Inc.
375 Hudson Street, New York, New York 10014, U.S.A.
Penguin Group (Canada), 10 Alcorn Avenue, Toronto, Ontario,
Canada M4V 3B2 (a division of Pearson Penguin Canada Inc.);
Penguin Books Ltd, 80 Strand, London WC2R 0RL, England;
Penguin Ireland, 25 St Stephen's Green, Dublin 2, Ireland
(a division of Penguin Books Ltd); Penguin Group (Australia),
250 Camberwell Road, Camberwell, Victoria 3124, Australia
(a division of Pearson Australia Group Pty Ltd); Penguin Books India Pvt Ltd,
11 Community Centre, Panchsheel Park, New Delhi - 110 017, India;
Penguin Group (NZ), cnr Airborne and Rosedale Roads, Albany,
Auckland 1310, New Zealand (a division of Pearson New Zealand Ltd);
Penguin Books (South Africa) (Pty) Ltd, 24 Sturdee Avenue, Rosebank,
Johannesburg 2196, South Africa

Penguin Books Ltd, Registered Offices:
80 Strand, London WC2R 0RL, England

Published by Dutton, a member of Penguin Group (USA) Inc.

First printing, May 2005
1 3 5 7 9 10 8 6 4 2

Copyright © 2005 by Jenny McCarthy
Illustrations by Grant Pominville (www.artbygrant.com)
All rights reserved

 REGISTERED TRADEMARK—MARCA REGISTRADA

LIBRARY OF CONGRESS CATALOGING-IN-PUBLICATION DATA
McCarthy, Jenny, 1972–
    Baby Laughs : the naked truth about the first year of mommyhood /
Jenny McCarthy.
        p. cm.
    ISBN 0-525-94883-X (alk. paper)
    1. Infants—Humor. 2. Motherhood—Humor. 3. Mothers—Humor.
I. Title.
    PN6231.I5M33 2005
    306.874'3'0207—dc22

                                                             2004065666

Printed in the United States of America
Set in ITC Garamond
Designed by Kathryn Parise

This book is printed on acid-free paper. ♾

To John—

thank you for loving me during my roughest times
and for being supportive through my hormonal roller coasters.
thank you for being an amazing father to our son and for
making me still feel sexy even though my ass had more
cheese on it than a Wisconsin cheese farm.
I love you, baby . . .

Contents

Contents

Contents

Contents ✺

Acknowledgments

To my mother . . . I know you really blew out your vagina giving birth to me. If I knew then what I know now, I would have tried to crawl out through your ear canal. Thanks for pushing so hard!!

To my sisters . . . Thank you for supporting me during my delivery by making disgusting faces and shaking your heads in horror. Thanks for being my wall of strength.

To my illustrator, Grant . . . dude, you are so freaking talented. Thank you for giving extra baby laughs to the new mommies who could use some.

Last but not least, to my son, Evan. I love your laugh. I love your stinky feet. I love putting bubbles in your hair. I love the way you look at me and I promise you I will love you until the end of time.

Move Over, Mrs. Cleaver!
There's a New Bitch in Town!

(Mommyhood)

I'm so excited to be a mom, and I hope you are too!! It's without a doubt the coolest, greatest, and most fulfilling thing that has ever happened to me. Has it been hard? Yeah, of course, but it's a GREAT hard. There are so many rewards to this kind of hard. I said in my last book that, after my delivery, I would do it all over again in a second. And I tell you this: After my baby's first year, I would do it all over again in a second.

I'm sure you've run into those people who try to scare you with horror stories. People would tell me in my ninth month that my life was going to be over. I hated hearing that I wasn't going to be able to do anything anymore. My freedom was gone. But know what I tell them now? My life isn't over . . . it's only just begun!

I can't believe it took me twenty-nine years of life to finally bring my son into this world. Am I glad I waited? OF COURSE! But I can't imagine how the world even survived without this precious little spirit being here. He's made me a better person. I realize what's important in life now, and I can't wait to spoil him with love.

People always say that the love of your child is so much different from any other kind of love. I would always say, "Yeah, yeah, I love my mom so much that I'm sure it's not that far off." But it is. It's not that it's more or less love, it's just that it consumes every part of your DNA. This baby is part of you. This baby will love YOU unconditionally, and it's up to YOU to mold this child into a beautiful being.

Wow, I sound all spiritual and shit. Hey, it happens! While you read this book, I might just take you to that spiritual place, but for the most part I'll be making you laugh your ass off. There are plenty of Baby Laughs you'll get to experience on your own. In the meantime, I hope you enjoy mine and learn a little something along the way.

Welcome to the new club, girls. The First-Year Mommy Club. But it's a new millennium, ladies, and it's our duty to make moms even better. So dig in and enjoy the book, cuz as I said before, "Move over, Mrs. Cleaver, there's a new bitch in town!" And this bitch is gonna make sure moms across the world look damn good!!

Blowing Out Your Vagina

(Vaginal Delivery)

I thought I was really funny in my last trimester telling people I was only three weeks away from "blowing out my vagina." Little did I know that my own slang term was the reason why I started hyperventilating during labor. When they told me I was fully dilated, I freaked. I pictured my vagina looking like a firecracker when I was finished. Just blown out, with pieces hanging off.

Anyway, when the nurses told me to start pushing, I

unwillingly did. I pushed extra hard just to get it over with. And if you were a good girl and read my last book, you know that I pushed and pushed and pushed and nothing happened. I knew something was wrong with my vagina, and so did the five doctors with their arms, not hands, but ARMS up my vagina. If a baby wasn't coming through this way, the doctors did a really great job stretching things out down there for no reason. By this point, which was a few hours into it, my strong and supportive husband started complaining of chest pain. If you could believe it, the doctor actually pulled him out of the room and had him tested to make sure he wasn't having a heart attack. I never told him this, but I was so exhausted I didn't even notice he was gone. Fortunately, he didn't have a heart attack and came back to chant *Push!* with the rest of the squad.

After I did even more pushing, the doctor started pulling out "toys." He pulled out the Hoover vacuum and tried sucking the baby out. I remember the doctor's arms shaking from using all his strength to yank out the baby. It looked like a tug of war. Next they tried using those giant salad spoons to try to get him out. Those things were so big I couldn't believe they just slid right in. The way they were bringing things in and out of my vagina was freaking me out. It got to the point where I thought the doctor was going to tell me he'd be right back, and then

he'd crawl inside me to check on things and I would just see his feet sticking out. I'm amazed that a vagina can open up like that. It's really not something to be that proud of, though. "Mine is bigger than yours" is not a goal for women.

If you haven't delivered yet and I'm totally freaking you out, I can tell you one great thing about all of this. I didn't feel a thing!! My epidural was working so well that you could have valet parked some cars up there, and I still wouldn't have felt anything. So, after three and a half hours of pushing, I was rushed in for an emergency C-section, which you'll read about in the next chapter.

When the baby finally does come through vaginally, most women say the discomfort factor goes way down, like taking the biggest but cutest #2 in your life. Aah!! While you're holding your baby and counting to make sure all of its fingers and toes are there, your doctor goes back to work on your sinkhole. If you tore, you might notice him doing some needlework down there. This is when the doctor cracks that joke, "And one more stitch for the husband." That's supposed to imply, of course, that he's making things tighter down there for your husband's pleasure. Whatever.

That's something my husband would always tease me about when I was pregnant. When I would tease him about blowing out my vagina, he would tease me back by saying that sex with me was going to feel like he was throwing a hot dog down a hallway.

I did ask my doctor if a woman's vagina kind of snaps back into place. He says that, for the most part, it really does after the first baby, but when you're getting up there with the number of deliveries, things can get a little blown out, and that some women opt for surgery to tighten it up down there. No, thanks, Doc, I'd rather just fake my orgasms and talk dirty than go through vagina-tightening surgery.

Another aftershock of delivery is noticing that when you sneeze or laugh hard you'll pee. That's true for a lot of women. I've tinkled from a good chuckle, but after de-livery I continued those annoying Kegels, which helped strengthen my control again.

The day after your delivery or even later that same day, I highly suggest asking for the numbing spray and an ice pack. My friends who actually tore described it as feeling like somebody had scrubbed the hell out of their "kitty" with a pad. They said it stung. So get an ice pack on that thing and ask for that numbing spray. It really does wonders. Right before you check out, ask for it again. A little squirt-squirt will make the bumpy ride home not so bumpy.

So, you officially did it. You officially blew out your vagina by this point, and all you got was a baby. I'm just kidding. Your suffering paid off because you are now going to experience the best of what life has to offer. I promise you. It truly is an amazing ride.

Hey, Dude!
Easy with That Scalpel!

(C-section)

After three and a half hours of pushing, it was no surprise to me that my baby's heart rate dropped by half and they sped me off for an emergency C-section. They numbed my body and held up what appeared to be a nail. The doctor kept poking it into different parts of my body, asking me if I felt anything. I repeatedly said no, and that's when they brought out the knife.

They sliced me open and went to work. Sitting next to

me with a look of fear on his face, my husband kept rubbing my head. His expressions got worse as the nurses kept shouting that they were losing the baby's heart rate. Then I felt the doctor, with great gusto, reach his hand and arm in and pull the baby out. I let out a huge moan because I felt enormous pressure on me and then, within seconds, my baby was free.

My world collapsed as I saw my husband's face turn pale. The baby was blue and not breathing. I asked what was wrong and my husband just shook his head in confusion. They quickly moved the baby to the other side of the room, where they tried desperately to get him to inhale. They slapped his back repeatedly and gave him oxygen.

At this point, I didn't know how long he was oxygen-deprived. All I knew was that I wanted him to breathe, and that if he had suffered any damage because of this insane delivery, I didn't care. I just wanted my baby to be alive. When he finally started to breathe, I cried and made so many pacts with God that I really should be the next Mother Teresa in a hut somewhere helping children.

They wrapped my baby up and brought him over to me. My husband and I were in awe that this miracle was ours. I couldn't do much except touch his cheek with my finger because I was pretty much paralyzed. But that didn't really matter. I had so much love wrapping around this kid that I knew he felt it. I'll also never forget the look on my husband's face. It was as if he had just caught a glimpse into heaven. Better yet, he was holding a piece of it.

Moments later, the nurses dragged my husband and my baby away, leaving me there to get sewed up. I remember feeling extremely nauseated at this point. I was so worried I was going to throw up while I lay on my back that I used every bit of energy I had left to prevent it. Until . . . one of the nurses approached me with a tin pan and said, "Would you like to see the placenta?"

I didn't have enough time to scream the word *NO!* I took one look at the placenta and hurled all over. What the hell was she thinking? I didn't belong to any tribe where we celebrated the placenta and gave it its own name. It was slimy and purply and I was grateful that they didn't force me to take it home.

Before they wheeled me out of surgery, the anesthesiologist shot me up with a big fat dose of morphine. I looked at him and smiled and said, "You are the chosen one."

He smiled back, and they pushed me into recovery. Let me just tell you that I was not in recovery with other preggers who had given birth. I was there with gunshot victims and anybody else who crawled the dirty streets of L.A. As they pushed me next to some guy moaning loudly, I begged them to take me to my room. The nurse told me that they wouldn't release me until I was able to move the lower half of my body. As soon as she said those words, I lifted the entire lower half of my body into the air. Her eyes almost fell out of her head.

It was one of those miracle moments of strength because, as soon she walked away, I couldn't move a muscle. I wanted to get out of recovery so badly that I channeled some strength that probably could have moved mountains. I wanted to see my baby! I had worked so hard cooking him in my belly and getting him out that for them to separate us seemed CRAZY.

The nurse came back in and said they couldn't bring me down to my room until their shift change. I asked her when that would be. She replied, "Five hours."

I began crying and thought of different ways I could slither my body down the hallways to find my baby. I was fighting the morphine now because it was trying to make me sleep, but I didn't want to. I wanted to see my baby, damn it!!

Five hours later they brought me to my room and put my baby in my arms. I wept. No, I bawled. I hugged him and kissed him and then passed out. My body was forcing me, finally, to sleep, considering what I had been through.

The next day I was in so much pain. I had a pee bag connected to me that they wanted to remove. I begged them not to because that meant I had to get up and walk to the bathroom. They said that was the whole point. Ugh! I wanted that pee bag connected for at least a month. I couldn't imagine walking, which is exactly what they made me do after they disconnected me. It took me about twenty-five minutes to get to the bathroom, and I cried the whole way.

When we got there, the nurse and my husband changed my diaper. I didn't want my husband to see the bloody mess down there. My diaper looked like a horror movie. But I guess he'd seen worse over the past couple of days.

The next night I woke up around 3:00 a.m., shaking uncontrollably. I yelled for the nurse. I was so cold I felt like I was on top of Mount Everest in a G-string. The nurse came in with heated blankets and told me it was because of the anesthesia. I talked to other women who had C-sections, and we commiserated about how weird this part was. We all had the shakes BAD. Why didn't they warn us that was coming instead of letting us freak out, thinking we were having seizures? Well, leave it to me to be the one who tells ya. Consider yourself warned if you have a C-section.

After about five days I was released, but I honestly felt that I needed another week in the hospital. Those damned insurance companies need to undergo C-sections and see how well they function after someone cuts them in half. I managed to get home but still couldn't move around. It took about another week to recover. It helped that my mom was going to be with me for a few days. If you undergo a C-section, you have to ask for help. Don't think you're putting anybody out by asking. They won't know you need it unless you open your mouth and say something.

On the vanity side, I can tell you that my C-section scar healed pretty well. Unfortunately, I, like almost all women who undergo C-sections, was left with what some people call a "shelf." It's a clump of fat that kind of hangs over your incision. But I already have stretch marks everywhere, so I'll just add "fat shelf" to my list of baby souvenirs.

They do a good job these days of hiding the incision in your forest. The problem is you do have to leave it a little hairier down there to cover it. Who cares, right? Your husband is probably so desperate to get into that area that he would happily dig for days just to find it.

Nursing Nazi

(Bottle or Boob?)

Ahh, the breast. A beautiful mound of clumped fat that men can't seem to get enough of. Some are big, some are small, but after pregnancy they're big, round, and veiny. For years we've used them as flirtation tools and sometimes as play toys for our loved ones. But now they are called to duty!! So say good-bye to your "fun bags" for now and say hello to your new udders.

Breastfeeding is a touchy subject for some women. One thing I know is that it's personal. It's my boob and my business. Throughout my pregnancy, and maybe yours too, people would ask me if I would be breastfeeding. Even the checkout girl ringing up my groceries would ask, and so would other people I had never even met before. These boobs are mine and I'm not sharing!

Okay, now that it's just you and me, let's talk about my boobs. As I lay drugged up in my hospital bed trying to recover, a nurse came in to check on my breasts. She asked me if I was going to breastfeed, and I told her I didn't know because honestly I hadn't made up my mind yet. She told me she was going to send in a nurse to help me out. I slurred "Okay" and passed out.

When I opened my eyes, standing over me was a female nurse wearing black-rimmed glasses and a giant button with a red slash through a milk bottle. This was the Nursing Nazi!! All she was missing was a moustache. She went on to tell me about the benefits of breastfeeding. Needless to say she had this list below fully memorized and she told it to me with much authority.

Did you know that . . .

- breastfeeding can boost your child's intelligence?
- breastfeeding protects your baby from diarrhea, respiratory problems, and ear infections?

- breastfeeding may protect your child against obesity?
- breastfeeding protects preemies from infections and high blood pressure later in life?
- breastfeeding may protect your baby from leukemia?
- breastfeeding helps you lose weight?

Being the idiot I am, who always makes a joke out of everything, I stopped her in the middle of her list to ask, "Yeah, but can it lower my car insurance?"

She didn't find that funny. She wanted to know why I was having a hard time with this decision. And my reason was SOOO stupid but it was a concern for me. I was worried that because I had implants, breastfeeding might somehow harm my baby. I loved my little bird way too much to have Mommy's foreign objects taint his milk. The Nursing Nazi told me that my milk duct was a separate tube. It was protected from the implant or anything else. I still worried that implants were kind of new technology and that maybe not enough years had passed by for all effects to show up. With my luck, I would breastfeed and then hear on the news that implants caused children to grow a third leg.

I needed more time. The Nursing Nazi continued to pressure me. I had to think of a way to get rid of her, so I told her I just crapped myself. She stopped mid-sentence and stared at me. She pulled a pamphlet out of her pocket with an entire list highlighted and said she'd send someone in who took care of things like that. I waved good-bye and plopped my head back. I thought about everything she'd said, and I knew my concern was completely foolish but it was still MY concern. My milk hadn't come in so I knew I still had some time to think.

The next day a "normal" nurse came in and checked on my breasts. She told me she was going to bind them tightly because it would help with the pain if I chose not to breastfeed. I laughed at her and told her nothing could compare with my C-section pain and that I doubted the milk would hurt that much. She just smiled and told me to ice my breasts when I got home. I remember thinking she was overreacting. My boobs hurt every month when I got my period. I didn't need to put a bag of frozen peas on them then. So my cocky ass just sat there as she tightly bound my breasts. I told myself that when my milk came in I'd make my choice.

So, if you're still a pregger and you've made up your mind not to breastfeed, let the nurses know right away. Maybe you could get lucky and avoid the Nursing Nazi.

Waitress, Can You Bring Me the Check? I'm Gonna Take My Baby TO GO!

(Coming Home)

The day arrived when I could finally go home. I was both terrified and excited. The nurses seemed just as excited to get me the hell out of there. They like the turnover. You're in, you're out.

I knew they weren't going to wrap my baby up in tinfoil shaped like a swan and toss us to the curb, so I took my time. Having a C-section was really difficult. I still had a very hard time walking, so I was enjoying the last of the hospital's wonderful painkillers. Those things were great. I knew what it was like to be Courtney Love for a week.

While my husband was wrapping up the bill, I lay in bed and thought about how nervous I felt being the one in charge of my baby now. When you undergo a C-section, you're in the hospital for about five days, so you get a little accustomed to handing the baby over to a nurse when you need to rest. There were no nurses coming home with me. My mother was going to be there, and that was comforting, but I knew she would eventually have to fly back home to Chicago.

Before you leave the hospital, you need to ask every question you can possibly conjure up for the nurses. Let them show you how to change a diaper. Ask about feeding times or whatever you feel unsure about or any of the stuff you didn't understand in all the million baby books you've read. I was too much in a fog to think up questions, so I hope you remember to open your mouth and ask away!

This is also a great time to "borrow" a few items from the hospital. Make sure you grab that nose suction thing. I call it a booger sucker! This will come in so handy. It will be hard to find a good one like it, so be sure to "borrow" the hospital's. Also grab an extra baby blanket. They look so cozy and are already broken in. Another thing to stock up on are those maxi pads that are the size of mattresses. Make sure to "borrow" plenty of those, although I'm sure they won't want those back after you're done with them.

Finally it was time to put our baby in the car seat. This was truly a great moment. The car seat is the first thing your baby uses from your collection of shower gifts, and hearing that click of the buckle made us giggle as we loaded him into it. I would always laugh when I saw moms sitting in the backseat with their babies while their husbands drove up front, alone. I just thought it looked weird. I wanted to say, "Go sit with your husband! Your baby isn't going anywhere strapped in that seat."

So I swore I'd never do that, but as we were about to drive off, I opened the door and sat next to my baby in the backseat. I'm such a hypocrite. But as they say, until you walk in a mommy's shoes, you have no idea. Actually, I don't think that's a saying, but just go with it.

The whole way home, my husband drove ten miles per hour under the speed limit. I wish there was a special lane dedicated to new mommies or at least a special siren we could put on the car, screaming, "NEW BABY GOING HOME . . . GET OUT OF THE WAY."

When we pulled up to the front of the house, I had my mom go inside and grab the camera. I wanted the moment to be captured on film. Now, when I look back at that picture, I laugh. In my head I thought it was going to be the most beautiful picture known to mankind: husband and wife with child. Instead I look like I'm wearing clothes custom-made for a hippo with our son tucked so deeply into his car seat you can't even see his face.

We walked into the house, and I showed him his new home. This was going to be his safe bubble and I was there to make sure that no one popped it. I showed him all of the great stuffed animals in his room and all the other stuff he was going to have fun looking at once he could see.

As I looked down at that squished face, I started crying. I did it! This was my boy. I told him he was going to be so happy he picked me as a mom. I was gonna love him and support him no matter what he wanted to grow up to be . . . except a mime. . . . They just always freaked me out.

Everyone always says their babies grow up so fast. So I hope you'll take the time to treasure all these sweet moments. Not so far away are some pretty stinky ones. Pun intended!

Okay, Um . . .
Can Someone Quickly Explain
How to Raise a Human Being?

(Freaking Out)

Y ou're home. You settled back into the nest. Your mom has left, and it's just you, your husband, and the baby. YES!

You begin taking on the sole responsibility of caring for the baby. Okay, this is when I started to freak out. "Oh, my God!! It's just us? But how do we know what to do? My mom picked up where the nurses left off. How am I just supposed to take over?"

The amazing thing is you do eventually slide nicely right into parenting. Just not overnight.

When the baby starts crying, you go through your list of logical reasons. You try feeding him. Nope, that ain't it. Then you try changing his diaper. Nope, that ain't it. He's still crying. But why? How come? That's when a new mom becomes lost and confused.

Then you begin to analyze the cry. "Well, it doesn't sound like a pain cry, so I don't need to panic." Maybe he's cold, so you bundle him up. Nope, that ain't it either. You try just about everything until you come to the conclusion that sometimes they just cry.

If you end up having a colicky baby, know that you are not alone. My son wasn't colicky, but that doesn't mean that someday Baby #2 isn't going to be. Doctors still don't know why some babies get colicky. I personally think they're pissed off not being in the cozy womb. Now they have to get cold, hungry, and gassy, and they ain't happy.

I actually told God before my son was born that he could be born without a pinkie toe just as long as he wasn't colicky. I know that's horrible, but I didn't care. Colicky stories are scary. If you do get a colicky baby, know that they do eventually grow out of it. If I were you, and I could be someday, I'd make sure to read up on tips on how to deal with colic.

I do know this: Colicky or not, newborns like to be

wrapped up like a burrito. It makes them feel like they are back inside Mommy. I'd wrap my son up nice and snug, and I gotta tell ya, it did wonders. Make sure they teach you how to do it in the hospital. They know how to make a great burrito!

I remember trying to figure out the whole burping thing. I saw the nurses in the hospital hold babies up on their knees like ventriloquists holding dummies. I hadn't seen babies burped that way before. It was always over the shoulder. Anyhow, I imitated the nurses, with little pats on the back. And whaddaya know? BURP! It definitely sounded like this kid was my son.

Then, other times, when I would try to burp the baby, he wouldn't do it. This drove me nuts because I was scared to put him back into the crib for fear of choking.

So I would sit there *forever*, trying to get him to burp until I realized that sometimes babies just won't burp. My son seemed to do just fine through those burpless nights. But, of course, I still slept with one eye open the whole time.

When you are finally allowed to give your baby a tub bath, which is well after the cord has fallen off, it's kind of cute and messy all at once. I still say the kitchen sink is your best bet in the beginning. Babies are so tiny, and the kitchen sink is the perfect height for you. Just throw a towel down in there or a baby sponge to avoid slippage, and then *scrub-a-dub-dub.* As long as the temp is lukewarm, you will most likely find your baby LOVING it.

If you have a boy, get ready for your baby to pee in your mouth when you are about to put him in the tub. As soon as I put his little toe in the water his pee stream always got me. Fun!

One of my favorite things to do with my son at this early age was to rock him in the chair and watch him smile. Every book, mother, and doctor will tell you that your baby isn't smiling at this age. Well, they can all kiss my ass. If I want to say my baby is smiling and not having gas, then he's smiling. I honestly believe that.

I know a newborn's vision is not up to par yet, and they don't really look at you when they "smile," but just watch them. It's amazing. I personally think they're smiling at their guardian angels or at your relatives who might have passed. 'Cause if you believe in all that stuff, your baby probably just saw them, like, a few weeks ago. So when they pop up, they're like, "Hey, how's it going?" My son would smile and giggle so hard at the ceiling. It was comforting to think that maybe my grandpa was making him laugh.

I honestly think it takes about one month to get the parent system down. That first week is like cramming for a test, but after a few more you will at least feel in control. You'll look like shit, with armpit hair down to the floor, and have bags under your eyes. But at least you'll have peace of mind, knowing that you're becoming a great mommy!

Ouch, My Udders Hurt!

(Breastfeeding)

I had a horrible dream one morning that I was stuck in a cave surrounded by biting ants and other bugs that hissed. I remember them charging toward me and attacking me but attacking only my breasts. They were biting and stinging my boobs, and I was trying to scream in my dream except no sound would come out. Finally I forced myself to open my eyes and awaken from this horrible nightmare.

But when I did, I sat up and screamed at the top of my lungs. My breasts still felt like they were being eaten by ants because I was in sooooo much pain. I'm talking give-me-another-C-section-over-this-kind-of-pain pain.

I was scared to look down at my boobs because they felt so different that I thought there could very well be ants crawling on them. So I let only one eye peek down there. Then I opened the other eye and screamed another horrific mouthful of horror. My breasts looked like GIANT bowling balls. No, giant watermelons. No, Pamela Anderson's seventh boob job. No, bigger than that! I can't use enough words to describe how HUGE they were.

As my scream continued, my mom and my hubby came running into the room. They took one look at my boobs and put their hands over their mouths, laughing. I didn't think it was funny but they did.

My milk had finally arrived. Because I wasn't breastfeeding yet, my boobs were forced to fill to the max with milk. I either had to jump on the breastfeeding bandwagon or go through a couple of days of severe drying up. I thought again about breastfeeding and how great the benefits were, but I was still so unsure about having implants in there that I decided against it. This really shows how ignorant I am, but hey, I'm blond and a cheerleader at heart. Sometimes we live up to our stereotype.

Anyway, when I got out of bed I immediately went to

the mirror and unwrapped my boobs, which had been bound by the nurses, and stared at them in "udder" dismay. I couldn't believe that they had morphed into these giant melons. They started at my collarbone and curved down to my mid-belly. The sides were so swollen that I could barely put my arms down. I went to walk into the kitchen to get a bag of frozen peas to ice them and screamed yet again. Any movement caused my breasts to violently attack me with pain. Now I got the whole "binding" thing. It caused less movement, which caused less pain.

Just because I was letting my milk dry up didn't mean I didn't leak for days on end. I was sitting watching *Oprah* with my mom and she said, "Oh, Jenny," and I said, "I know, Oprah's haircut is the one you were talking about."

She said, "No, honey, look at your boobs."

I looked down and saw that I had leaked through my shirt. BAD!! It was the grossest wet T-shirt contest ever. So I got up to take a shower (because that milk is so sticky) and when I got in, the hot water surrounded my breast and milk started squirting out like it was a showerhead. It seemed as if there wasn't just one hole where milk was squirting out, but MANY holes. I was giving the walls of my shower their very own milk bath. That freaked me out.

The next day I was standing in the living room talking

with my mom, and a cat commercial came on the TV. The cat was singing, "Meow meow meow meow," waiting for some food. Again my mom said, "Oh, Jenny," and I said, "I know, that's a pretty ugly cat."

Again she said, "No, look at your boobs."

I looked down and saw that not only did I leak through my shirt but there were two puddles of milk on the floor. The damn cat meowing caused my boobs to leak. I had no idea that outside influences could do that. I guess I associated cats with drinking milk, and so it happened. *Squirt-squirt!*

Once it even happened in the grocery store when a woman walked by with her crying baby. *Squirt-squirt!!* Ugh! That was so embarrassing. I tried to cover up my leak circles with loaves of bread. They were the only things long enough to cover the streaks down my shirt. They do sell leakage pads for women's breasts, but sometimes that isn't enough.

My friends who were breastfeeding would talk about how they had such a hard time getting their kids to latch onto the nipples. It helps if you make your choice in the hospital so the nurses can show you how to do it. Other friends of mine found breastfeeding harder than pregnancy, especially in the beginning when a baby eats every two hours. You don't get much sleep at all. But they did say it was such a beautiful bonding experience that they would do all those sleepless nights again for the well-being of their babies. Boy, don't I feel like an asshole. I do plan on breastfeeding next time, though.

Another thing moms talk about is what happens to their breasts after they stop breastfeeding. This is not meant to freak you out. I just need to be honest about it so you don't go in blind. Breastfeeding can make your nipples possibly bleed and dry up, causing them to crack a bit. Some moms say they wound up with permanent nipple hard-on. They do sell nipple moisturizer, so I highly suggest splurging on some.

I've also heard women call their boobs "zucchinis" because they hang down like long squashes when you complete your breastfeeding mission. "Pancake boobs" is another slang favorite, because some women's breasts become flat and deflated. If you open up any *National Geographic*, you'll see plenty of pancake boobs. It's just another part of our bodies that we surrender for the well-being of our children. See what I get to look forward to next time?

So, make sure you read up on all the positive effects of breastfeeding, and if you choose not to breastfeed, don't let others make you feel guilty. Just know that when you see the Nursing Nazi headed your way, run like hell or crap in your bed. Either one should keep her away.

I'll Take the Twelve-Pack of Spit Rags, Ten Boxes of Diapers, Seven Packets of Onesies, the #1 Approved Car Seat—and Throw That Super-Deluxe 2010 Stroller in Too!

(Overbuying and Stroller Envy)

Just when you think you have EVERYTHING, Junior is born, and you feel like you have NOTHING. I don't care if you're Gwyneth Paltrow, with all the money in the world, if you're a new mom, you're going to find yourself making many trips to the store. In fact, the cashiers at Target are going to start greeting you by your first name, and you're going to respond with, "Hey, Sara, how's it going?"

Within the first month of bringing your baby home, you're going to realize that everyone at your shower bought you things like baby booties with bows on them instead of the essentials. Let's face it, your aunts know that no one is going to "Ooh" and "Ahh" over a box of diapers and baby wipes. The shower is their moment to show off. They want to feel proud as everyone watches you hold up the handmade cross-eyed angel with the inscription *God Bless This Baby*. Which is why, months later, you keep seeing new moms running to the store in panic.

When you find yourself in this situation, you're going to feel the need to overbuy. Don't! I'll tell you why. Your newborn will grow out of things within days. I'm not joking. You're going to want to buy eleven cases of diapers, but your baby will outgrow them by the time you've used the first few boxes. The same goes for onesies. You'll be stocking up on them constantly because you're throwing them away like paper towels. Between the poops and the spit-ups, no detergent on earth is strong enough to get them clean.

As you frantically search the aisles, you will face yet another crisis—choosing which brand to buy. It's so HARD!!! You, like me, will be staring at ten different brands of bottles and other baby items, not really certain which is best. Do you go for the brand that's on sale? But then you think, "If it's on sale, does that mean it's not safe?" No one can tell you which brand is best because all babies are different. You might get lucky, but for the most part, your baby will be the one to dictate the brand you use. After going through five different brands of bottles, I wound up with the cheapest because those were the ones my son responded to. They were the last ones I tried because the bottles were so ugly, with pictures of raccoons and ferrets on them. They almost looked like I got them at a garage sale. But they were the bottles he liked best, so that's what I stuck with.

After you get a consistent buying pattern for your essentials, you will notice that some of the items you already have—things you bought or received at your shower, like your stroller—don't work as well as you were hoping. Even worse, you might stroller your baby to the park and notice that everyone else has a prettier baby stroller than you do. Then panic will set in—soon, everywhere you go, all you'll see are moms pushing their beautiful strollers while yours looks like it's made of cardboard. This symptom is called stroller envy. It's inevitable.

Even if you think your stroller is the best money can buy, it's not. Someone will always have a better stroller than you do. Men show off their cars. Women show off their strollers. Even celebrity moms are guilty of it. They know damn well that pictures are being taken of them with their $5,000 strollers. I'm not exaggerating. I think it's ridiculous!!

My stroller cost $150, and I used it until the wheels were falling off. I might have been envious of those celebrities, but I'm not stupid. There are plenty of perfectly good strollers out there for a decent price.

So don't panic, ladies. Just remember to experiment with brands and not to let cute baby commercials make your buying decisions for you. And when stroller envy kicks in, just choose one that works, and don't worry if you can't afford the air-conditioned model with the flat-screen TV.

The Headless Penis

(To Cut or Not to Cut)

AHH, the penis. What would women do without them? I've always been fascinated with how they look. They're either big, small, narrow, stubby, purple, or veiny. And always anxious to please. The first time I ever saw one I was horrified. I think I was sixteen, and I remember wondering how in the hell could men even deal with walking around with all that meat and potatoes between their legs. I was so grateful to have a vagina. As I grew older I became less weirded out by penises, of course, but I still found their man-junk fascinating!

It took me until college to be introduced to my first "uncut" penis. What does every girl do after seeing her first uncircumcised penis??? She calls all of her friends and tells them she just saw one—in those early dating years, at least. I don't think I'd call anyone now. In fact, people would probably be weirded out if I did. Anyway, the majority of my friends and I knew men usually had circumcised penises. So does my husband. Needless to say, when it was time to make a decision to cut or not to cut, I didn't hesitate. "Like father, like son," right?

If you don't know what an uncircumcised penis looks like, you will once your baby boy is born. When I saw my son's for the first time, I thought it looked kind of like a wrinkled French fry. I had the hardest time knowing that I would have to be the one to tell the doc, "Go ahead and take that knife and slice some skin off. AHH!" It seemed so cruel. I was in such an emotional state that this choice was KILLING me. I created this beautiful bun of love! How could I do anything to cause him pain?

But I did, and my main reason was stupid, but truthful. I wanted him to have a pretty penis. I always thought the cut ones were prettier, but some disagree. That's fine. A lot of people make the decision to cut because a circumcised penis is easier to keep clean. The guy won't have to lean it over the bathroom sink for a pull-back and rinse. But is it morally wrong to have your kid go through circumcision just to have what YOU consider a pretty penis?

Okay, right now my husband is standing over my shoulder reading this, shouting, "Stop calling it a pretty penis! Our son is going to be embarrassed. Call it a battle sword or something!"

So his "battle sword" was now scheduled for its first battle. My doc insisted on waiting a week. I thought that was CRAZY. I didn't want to wait a week. I wanted it done while the baby and I were still in the hospital. That way, if anything went wrong, we were in the right place. Also the nurses could help him recover properly. My doc said that it was healthier to wait in case of an infection because he'd be stronger to fight it. Ugh! Fine, I waited.

The day we took him into my gyno's office will be burned into my head forever. I held my son tightly on the elevator ride and told him how sorry I was to put him through this. But hopefully his wife someday would appreciate what I was doing. Feeling still very emotional due to high volumes of hormones running through my body, I walked down the hallway like someone was shouting DEAD PENIS WALKING! I burst into tears and almost bowed out. My husband gave me a pep talk to dig in deep and be strong for my boy.

We headed into a room and the nurse pulled out a molded piece of plastic to fit the baby's body that included straps for his arms and legs, just like the electric chair. So, what did Mommy do when she saw this? Screamed "AHHH!!!!" And ran out of the room and sobbed down the hallway!!! I left my husband in there with my son. I couldn't be there to witness it. I sat on a bench, plugged my ears, and started saying the "Our Father." I figured Jesus was Jewish, so he could relate.

A few minutes later the door opened up, and my husband walked out with our baby in his arms. My son was crying hard, and my husband looked pale after watching the procedure. The doctor told me how to care for the cut, which was to put an enormous amount of Vaseline on the penis with every diaper change. This was so the diaper wouldn't stick to the booboo and tear it open. A great piece of advice I can give you is to buy the Vaseline in a tube that squirts out. That way you can just squirt it around the penis instead of having to rub it on.

As soon as I got home that day I gave my son a good ounce of Tylenol and placed him in his crib. He was exhausted and rightly so. I stared at my boy and rubbed his back. All I could do was tell him I was sorry and that

Mommy was doing her best to take care of his "battle sword."

But, circumcised or uncircumcised, just know that your son, like most men, is going to love his penis no matter what you decide.

Rock Star Lullabies

(Noisy Influences)

Rocking your baby for the first time at home is truly a beautiful experience. For months you searched for that perfect rocker. Something that looked pretty but also cushioned your fat ass. No more imagining holding your baby as you rock. This is your moment. You have arrived!

When I sat down with my baby for the first time, I caressed him and cried. I stared at those beautiful features and began the back-and-forth rocking motion in my chair like good moms do. I wanted him to feel safe and loved, so I snuggled him close. It was such a beautiful intimate moment, just the two of us. Mother and child in pure bliss.

I wanted to make this moment even more magical and sing my son a beautiful lullaby. So I began. . . . *Hush little baby, don't say a word, mama's gonna buy you a lullaby and if that mockingbird dies* . . . Wait, that's not right. I tried a different one. . . . *Twinkle twinkle, little star, how I wonder what you're doing tonight?* . . . No, damn . . . I don't know any of the words. I prepared for everything else during my pregnancy, but I didn't prepare for this. I sounded like a jackass ruining this beautiful moment. So, I dug in deep and gave it another shot. . . . *You know Prancer and Dancer and Donna and Nixon.* Damn it!!! That's not it!!!

I felt so stupid. What was wrong with me? How could I not know the words to these classics?? I had been watching too much MTV and VH1 during my pregnancy. I looked down at my little baby and smiled. He just wanted to hear the sound of my voice, not necessarily the words. I just had to figure out a song I knew the words to. Then it came to me . . . so I began. . . . *Oops I did it again, I played with your heart, got lost in the game, oh baby,*

baby. . . . I did it!!!! And my song even had the word baby in it!!

I was on a roll after that. Britney was followed by Madonna, Barry Manilow, and Elton John. I even threw some Metallica in there to beef up my son's testosterone after singing him one too many Barry songs.

Speaking of music, you might have received or heard about music CDs for your baby. Some to go to sleep to, some to sing along to, and other type of noisemakers that make sounds like the baby is still in the womb. I had heard and read that these CDs could help your baby get to sleep easier but they were only a "short-term solution." Your baby eventually needs to learn how to fall asleep on his own. Great! Another thing to wean him off!

But I gave the CDs a shot. And that lasted all of a week. I was always so tired by the time I put my baby to sleep that I didn't even have the energy to press play on the CD player. My son did just fine not listening to whales mating in the ocean. Until, of course, the day that Satan's mutt took up residence in our neighbor's yard. I don't mind a garbage truck, an airplane, or even a police siren zooming by. But this was a bark that resonates through your whole body and NEVER ends.

First of all, people who don't have children or want children usually have pets as their children. Come on, we've all met that person who says, "You want to see a picture of my baby?" And then pulls out a picture of a three-legged cat. So immediately I knew that these neighbors would be tough.

The first attempt was sending my husband next door to tell them that our newborn's window is next to their dog run and to try to minimize the barking. Flash forward to *BARK BARK, RUFF RUFF!!* Followed by *WAA WAA* from my son. Okey-dokey! Now what?

Next, I decided to personally take my crying baby over there and show them what Satan's pet was doing to my child. No answer! But I knew they were home! Hmmm, how would they like a nice poo-poo diaper in the mailbox? Maybe then they'd answer. As much as I wanted to, I didn't.

Instead for the next week or so my husband and I kept screaming *SHUT UP* over the fence. Still nothing. Then we bought them a dog collar that has an anti-barking electrocution device on it and put a red ribbon around it. Still NOTHING. I could hear them as they opened it. "Would they put an anti-crying collar around THEIR baby?" UGH! It was driving me nuts. It was just one more thing on my list that made us finally sell our house and move. Not the only reason, but definitely one of the reasons.

I was close to completing all of our packing as my husband and I joked around about how we'd like to play

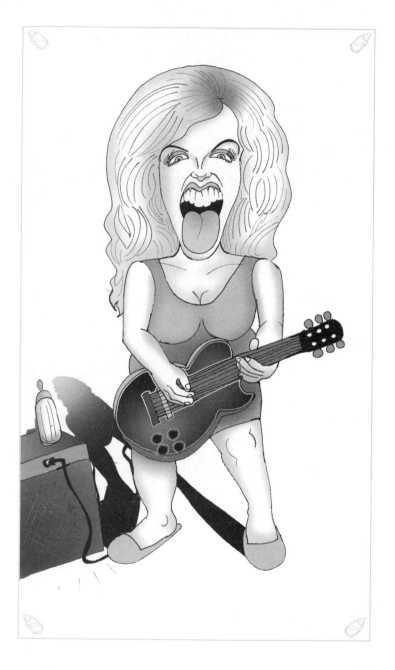

one last game of kickball on our street, using the dog as the ball. I know that's mean, but when you're sleep deprived, you get delirious. Soon after this, I was watching TV while my husband was out and saw on the news that someone had poisoned a neighbor's dog. My eyes bugged out, and I ran outside in my PJs, terrified that Satan's pet was already buried, "Oh no," I thought. "I drove my husband to commit doggie murder!!"

I was so terrified that my husband had given the dog a farewell cookie, I jumped up on the fence and looked over. There he was, Satan's pet, going apeshit on me. *RUFF RUFF, BARK BARK.* I was so happy to hear the bastard, I didn't care if he woke the baby. I simply smiled, gave the dog the finger, and moved ten miles away.

Because drama followed by comedy seems to hover over me wherever I go, you should all get a kick out of knowing that I moved into a house that has four dogs next to my son's window. Yes, the drama continues. I'm trying to figure out the name of this chapter in my next book. Is it . . . *FETCH THIS, BITCH!* or *TASTE MY CYANIDE SAUSAGE?* Yes, that will be available in hardcover only.

So, no matter what the noise is, your bad singing, stupid whale CDs, or Satanic dogs in the neighborhood, just know that making the best out of a bad situation is really the only thing you can do.

Ew! It Looks Like a
Burnt Cocktail Wiener!

(Losing the Umbilical Cord)

I can honestly say that every body part of your baby is the most beautiful thing in the world . . . except for the dried-up umbilical cord. I remember the first time I saw my baby's clipped up in the hospital. It didn't look like a burnt cocktail wiener . . . YET. It looked more like a noodle. No big deal. I just felt intrigued by it, amazed that this little cord had been the link to my baby's survival and that now he'd cut loose from me to experience this crazy world filled with germs and bad people that I have NO CONTROL OVER. (Sorry, I was feeling a bit emotional for a sec.)

My husband was sad that his only duty in the delivery was over. Prior to delivery, he would describe to me how he was going to cut the cord so it wouldn't be too long and would be a clean cut. The practice paid off. It was a good cut. He said it felt like cutting a tough sausage. I say wiener, he says sausage. At least you can tell we think alike.

During your pregnancy you might have heard or read about cord-blood banking. They say that cord blood is a great source of stem cells that could save lives. I was really into it, but I just never got around to banking the blood. But I think I will next time. If it's something that interests you and you're still pregnant, do something about it now. Once they cut the cord you can't ask them to throw it in a Ziploc baggy to take it home with you.

The day you take your baby home, you'll notice that taking care of the cord is yet another task that you will have to figure out. For years doctors have told moms to put rubbing alcohol around the belly button to help dry it up and keep it clean. Being the prepared pregger that I was, I was ready for this and stocked up on the rubbing alcohol. Well, wouldn't ya know it??!! My doctor told me it was no longer necessary. But Target had alcohol on sale and I had already stocked up on it, damn it! That doesn't surprise me, though. I've always been the one who was a few years behind everyone else and also never on time in the fashion world. For instance I JUST GOT the fashionable Jennifer Aniston haircut that was really popular in 1995. But don't fret if your doctor tells you to use rubbing alcohol. Many still do. And mothers and mothers-in-law are the first to insist that you DO!

One very useful tip to avoid irritating the cord while changing the baby is to fold the diaper down so it won't rub against the cord. The last thing you want to do is accidentally get rid of it before its time. You are also not allowed to get it wet, which is why you are constantly wiping your baby down with a rag instead of giving him tub baths. They say to avoid those for at least ten days after it's fallen off.

You can expect the cord to fall off in ten to twenty-one days, but I think it took all of a week and a half or so for it to start turning black. Which was SOOOO GROSS!! You could do what my husband and I did to make it less gross and more funny, which was making up different names for it. Like . . . the dead toe, Charlie the charcoal nub, the frostbit thumb, and my personal favorite, Gary Coleman.

Then it happened!! I was changing my baby's diaper and the little sucker flew across the room. Not on its own, of course. I slid his diaper against it, and it broke right off and hit the wall. I screamed like bloody hell in fear that I'd just ripped off a body part.

I slowly walked toward the cord and picked it up. There it was, all by itself, in all of its glory, no longer attached to my son. Charlie the charcoal nub was out there to face the world on its own. A world that's full of germs and bad people. Yes, that's right, I became attached to this little black nub. I couldn't just throw it away.

Now what? I opened the drawer full of shower gifts, hoping someone gave me a special frame meant for the umbilical cord. But OF COURSE there was nothing. I had to be the only idiot who felt something for a dead cord and wanted to hang it up. So I knew what had to be done. I called my husband into the room. I thought he would come join me and pay his respects and then together we would let it go. But instead he took it and flushed it right down the toilet. I watched it circle the toilet and waved. "Good-bye, little guy. Thanks for everything."

And, of course, I cried. Postpartum was in full swing!!! I still kinda miss the cord. So just keep it dry and your little black nub will be off in no time.

THIS CHAPTER IS DEDICATED TO CHARLIE THE CHARCOAL NUB

THE HARDWORKING CORD

08/2001–05/2002

I'm Singing the Mommy Blues

(Postpartum Depression)

Postpartum depression is no laughing matter. It's real, it's ugly at times, and I'm so glad that people and even celebrities are talking about it. Every single woman experiences postpartum differently. It's yet another hormonal obstacle that new moms have to get over and always eventually do. Sometimes postpartum depression lasts a few weeks and sometimes a few months. And if you're lucky, maybe you won't get it at all.

The great thing is knowing that it's not in our heads, and there is now plenty of information offered to us. I prepped myself so I was fully aware of what might happen to me. Just reading up on postpartum depression made me feel like I was already in control of it, but I was still scared.

About a week and a half or so after delivery, I noticed that I had a sinking sadness inside my chest. To give you a little bit of an idea, I would say it's just like the depression you get when you have PMS—ya know, like when you're driving in the car and hear that Barry Manilow song and just start bawling your eyes out. That is EXACTLY the same kind of sadness, just multiplied by a digit or two.

I felt really, really sad. It was as if someone told me about a death of an old acquaintance—that kind of feeling—but I had no reason to be sad. I just was. In the next day or so, I noticed that my excitement about my baby had kind of worn off. His cry wasn't as cute as it had been a week before. I knew then that postpartum depression had arrived, and I didn't want to fight it. I put my seat belt on and told myself to surrender to the feeling, hoping that the ride would be a smooth one.

I told my husband about my feelings, and as I went about my day, he had one eye watching me. He had heard stories about women who hurt their babies and didn't know if I was going to go off the deep end. But I told him not to worry that much and assured him that I was fine. I didn't have those destructive types of feelings. Just sadness, that was all.

Then a magnet that was holding up a piece of paper on the refrigerator fell off, and I dropped to the ground in tears. The way the paper fell was so beautiful and graceful that I couldn't help crying about it. In fact, anything that looked beautiful or caused me even a little bit of emotion drove me to tears. I remember going outside to look at a rainbow in the sky and noticed that it was only half a rainbow, not a full one. So I cried. I cried when the cashier asked me if I wanted my milk in a bag. I cried over Oprah's new set. Anything, really, drove me to tears.

One night I had a wave of overwhelming emotion that made me wake my baby up and rock him. I loved him so much that I held him tight and wept and wept and wept. I had this overwhelming surge of love and feelings of finally having a true purpose in life and that was to populate the world with my children. I just wanted to make babies. Lots of them. I was obviously really good at it and I knew I was going to be a great mom so I would raise incredible human beings to spread love and happiness around the world.

I told my mom of my plan. She looked at me and fake-smiled. "Sure, honey, that's a great idea," she said.

But what her mind was saying was, "My daughter has completely lost it." She knew in a few days I would probably have reconsidered my new mission. She was right.

For about three weeks I wanted nothing to do with the rest of the world. I avoided all phone calls from my friends and didn't want anyone coming over to visit. This was strange for me because I'm a people person, yet I wanted to hide in my cave and not let anyone in. Feeling anxious or fearful is yet another symptom of postpartum depression.

My agent called and asked me if I wanted to think about going back to work yet. The thought just made me sick. I wanted no part of it. I wanted to live in my baby's room and sell Avon products over the phone. I was definitely not feeling back to my good old self.

There are times during this period when you might actually say to yourself, "What did I get myself into?" and even, "I'm just so not diggin' this." It's not that you hate your baby. It's just that having your emotions running wild and all of these new responsibilities can honestly make any new mom break down and cry. If your symptoms persist for more than three weeks, ask your doctor to test your hormone levels.

But if you ever feel like your roller coaster is making double and triple loops and you want to do any harm at all, please get help. You might have postpartum psychosis, which is rare but much more serious. No one will commit you. They will just commend you for being brave and speaking up. Remember, help is always there.

So, mommies, beware. Postpartum depression is a real thing. Be prepared for it, not scared of it, and you should get through it like the rest of us. If my crazy ass came back to reality, your crazy ass will too.

Hey, Buddy, It's Your Turn to Get Up with the Baby!

(Split Parenting)

Saying anything close to, "Hey, buddy, it's your turn to get up with the baby," could have gotten a woman in lots of trouble back in the bad old days. I'm so glad times have changed because I can assure you that I would have been the woman in the neighborhood who would have been hung in the town center, with her husband holding the rope.

If you are breastfeeding, the chances you will get up

with the baby are pretty much 100 percent. That is the case unless, of course, you pump and bottle the milk for your husband's tired ass to use in the middle of the night. Now, I know it's traditional for men to go to work to bring home the bacon and you're supposed to fry it up in a pan, but I am a firm believer that going to work is a lot easier than caring for a newborn. Most husbands I talk to agree with that comment. They say they feel bad when they shut the door in the morning, leaving their disheveled wives slumped on the couch burping the baby. So, if caring for the baby is harder, then a few times a week the man should do some night feedings. If there are any husbands reading this right now who disagree, they're probably calling me a bitch, but I would just tell them they would have to get in line behind all of my ex-boyfriends.

Anyway, more and more men are helping out these days, and I commend them for that. I change this diaper, you change the next. That should be all new moms' anthem. Yeah, right. My husband was unbelievably helpful, though. He really did help out more than I could even have begged. Sure, there were times when the baby would cry, and I would bribe him to do the feeding by saying I would owe him a B.J., like, six months from now. He was so desperate, he would agree.

Because we didn't hire any "night nurse" to do the

night feedings, my husband and I created a system that worked really well for us. I would go to bed at 8 or 9:00 P.M., and he would stay up and do the feedings until 2 or 2:30 in the morning and then I would take over. He would sleep until 7:30, allowing us both at least five hours of straight sleep. Sure, we were both still tired, but we didn't look like we were in *Night of the Living Dead*.

My son started sleeping through the night rather quickly, so we got lucky. I won't rub it in, so I'll tell you about my best friend, who had the hardest time ever getting her baby to sleep. As she put it, "My baby just doesn't sleep." All night he would be up and almost all day. She stopped breastfeeding and went to bottle-feeding in the hopes of changing his sleeping schedule. When ten months went by and her baby still didn't sleep, she looked like she might go hari-kari on someone. She made an appointment to see a sleep specialist, and found out her baby was overtired. She needed to put him down by 6:00 P.M. Guess what? It worked.

So, I hope your husband is a trouper and really gives you a helping hand. If not, tell him his hand will be the only thing he's going to be intimate with for a LONG time.

Damn It!
My Ass Is Bleeding Again!

(Hemorrhoids)

These little balloon-knot-looking, son-of-a-bitch, bloody pouches SUCK!! If you didn't have them during your pregnancy, your chances of having them after delivery are a lot greater. Especially if you had hours of endless pushing during delivery, like me. Hemorrhoids are almost like a little going-away present from Mother Nature. A little pouch to take home with you and burst open any time you please.

When you come home from the hospital, there is so much going on down there that you don't really know the hemorrhoids are there, UNTIL . . . you take your first poop. And even doing that, you're terrified because you're afraid any pushing you do is going to cause all of your insides to come out of your vagina because you are still a bloody mess down there on top of all the pain.

But I eventually had to poop, even though I waited a few extra days. So I took a seat and told myself to enjoy the ride. All I thought about was the pain from my incision while pushing, but then I began to feel a sharp pain in the bum-bum exit area, followed by an excruciating one. My face turned purple, and I screamed louder than anyone in California at that moment. The scream was followed by tears, as my husband came bursting into the bathroom to find me crying on the toilet. I knew those bastards were back with a vengeance!!

After that I was so terrified to go #2 that I avoided it altogether. I knew that the longer I waited, the more painful it was going to be. But I just wanted to make sure those "delivery hemorrhoids" were gone, or at least 90 percent healed before I sent a "tree" through them. So I waited and waited. About fifteen days came and went.

Then one night I began to scream yet again in my bedroom. As usual, my husband shouted, "What's wrong NOW?" I was crying and doubled over in pain, telling him my appendix had just blown up and that I had to go to the emergency room. He saw that I was in severe amounts of pain and rushed me there.

They took me right in and did an X-ray. I knew I was going to have appendix surgery, which sucked because I'd just had a C-section three weeks before!! But the doc came in and said, "Well, we know what's going on. You're full of shit."

I said, "I'm not making this up! I'm in pain. Why would I bullshit you?"

He said, "No, literally you're full of shit. Your intestines are filled rock solid with it."

I couldn't believe I was in this much pain because I was constipated. I told him I was scared to poo because of my hemorrhoids. He said that that was very common, but I was so embarrassed, especially when the doctor had me sign an autograph for his nephew at college after lecturing me about crapping. Ugh!

So they gave me a bottle of stool softeners. They were surprised the hospital didn't give me any after delivery. Yeah, me too! So I took my stool softeners, went home, and waited.

Then my moment arrived. It was time, and I was hoping that the hemorrhoids had healed. I'll spare you yet another bathroom story, but I'll tell you that though the stool softeners made things a little more pleasant, the hemorrhoids were back AGAIN!! I found myself investing in some Tucks medicated pads, and I must say they did take most of the discomfort away. Unfortunately, I was addicted to them. I would just stick one between the cheeks and go on my merry way. I even went shopping with a Tucks tucked in. I didn't care. I felt better. That's all that mattered.

Unfortunately, hemorrhoids still linger around my life. Kind of like an ex-boyfriend. They show up, and you still don't want anything to do with them, yet they keep coming back. My doc said you can have them removed with surgery. I don't think so. I just bought some extra stock in Tucks medicated pads. I'll see how long that will hold me. In the meantime, get yourself some stool softeners and take them after delivery to help soften the load. Literally!

Oh, No, I Ran Out of Cottage Cheese. Wait, I Can Just Scrape Some Off My THIGHS!

(Still FAT)

G reat, now I had NO excuse. I could no longer get away with saying things like "I'm not fat, I'm pregnant"; "No, silly, I'm just retaining a lot of water"; and "I need to eat all the leftovers because I'm eating for two."

The baby was now out of my body, and it was time to face a woman's ugliest reality . . . looking at her fat. This took a while to do, ya know. I avoided looking at my body altogether for about three weeks after I gave birth.

When I showered I would just pretend I was wiping down a hippo at the zoo, not my actual self. I refused to look in any mirror but knew the day was coming to face the grim reaper of fat. CELLULITE.

I finally started to feel like I was healing from my C-section. I officially stood up straight for the first time without being hunched over and felt like I might make an attempt to hit the gym in the near future. But I was RE-ALLY unmotivated. I just wanted to spend every second with my baby and not have to worry about hitting my target heart rate.

So I knew I needed a strong motivator. That was the day I decided to REALLY look in the mirror. This day will unfortunately be burned into the back of my head for the rest of my life. I took off my robe and turned on some overhead lighting (we all know from dressing rooms, overhead lighting was created by the devil). I opened my eyes and SCREAMED, "Oh MY GOD."

I didn't know what to cry about first. I still had two chins. I had purple, veiny, GIANT tits. Cottage cheese holes were dripping down my thighs, to the point that I couldn't see my knees, and the absolute, hands-down worst thing was the deflated tire around my waist, a jelly roll that jiggled and slapped each side of my body when I shook back and forth. I had a C-section scar with stitches that lined my abdomen, and cellulite divots that could

hold golf balls. I simply stood there and stared in awe at Mother Nature's artwork.

I was so glad my husband was not home to see the piglet monster. I just wish once in a man's lifetime he could experience what a woman has to go through to give birth. My husband hadn't seen me completely naked in months, and you could be damn sure he wasn't gonna start then.

Just when I thought things couldn't get any worse, I realized I hadn't looked at my ass yet!! I contemplated just avoiding it altogether, but I figured I had gone this far, why stop? So I turned, looked over my shoulder, and opened my eyes. I stared at it for a beat and, believe it or not, started laughing. Not because it didn't look that bad but because it was the largest, ugliest ass I had ever seen. It even had a few zits on it. The laugh eventually ended because I began to cry.

At this point I was really pissed off that I'd let myself gain so much weight. I guess I was in denial and kept thinking it was water weight as I shoved a pan of brownies in my mouth every night. When I got home from the hospital, I did manage to weigh myself to see how much was lost in delivery. I lost thirty pounds. Wow, sounds great, huh? Except for the fact that I still had to lose FIFTY more pounds!!!! I could clearly see at this moment that the scale wasn't broken like I thought it was.

I was now just too embarrassed even to walk into a gym. Especially with paparazzi around taking pictures of celebrities after they have babies to show how fat they got. It's such a horrible thing to do, but secretly I LOVE reading about how fat they got too. Now I kinda get why people like seeing celebrities get fat. Ya figure, hey, if we're struggling, they should too. But even though I loved reading about fat celebrities, I didn't want to be one. So I stayed home until I lost more weight. What a wuss, huh?

Still, sitting around at home for a couple more weeks did nothing. Later on in the book you will read about my journey toward losing the weight in "Burning the Muumuu"!! So, for now, have peace of mind, knowing that this mini-celebrity's ass is the size of the *Titanic* and it ain't going down that quick!

Introducing the TURDinator!

(Endless Shits)

There is nothing in this world like baby poop. The aroma, the ability to defy gravity, the texture, and my favorite . . . the color. I remember thinking, "Wow, I've never seen this type of green before." You hear other moms talk about it. Maybe even get some stories from your own mom. But when you get to experience it first-hand you'll realize there's nothing like it!

The first couple of poops will seem really adorable.

They don't even stink yet, so suck that fresh air in while you can. You even show your husband how cute his boy's little poo-poo is and wonder what all the fuss is about. "It's not THAT bad."

In the first few days after coming home from the hospital, I begged my husband to go deal with the 3:00 A.M. crying baby and that I'd get the next one. He rolled off the bed and did the zombie walk toward the baby's room. The next thing I hear is "HOLY SHIT" being shouted out across the house. Needless to say I sprang out of the bed and flew toward my son's room. I was shouting back, "WHAT? WHAT THE HELL IS WRONG?"

My husband was standing at the doorway with his mouth hanging open. He looked at me and said, "Our son just crapped a one-foot turd."

I pushed him out of the way and walked toward my baby. I looked at him and said, "That one-foot turd IS our baby!!"

Poop was covering my son head to toe. There was not one spot of clean pink skin. He did indeed look like a one-foot turd. This was the first time it had happened, and we were so panicked because we thought he could get an infection in his eyes or, even worse, maybe eat some poop off his hand. So we kept shouting at each other, "DO SOMETHING!!!"

But we didn't know where to begin, because where

DO you begin? There's crap everywhere. My husband un-buttoned my son's one-piece and pulled it over the baby's head.

Lesson #1: When you pull a one-piece that is full of poo over your baby's head, there will be even more poo smeared onto your baby's face—only this time guaran-teeing poop up the nostrils. Which is exactly what hap-pened! So I started screaming at my husband, "Look what you did." Of course I would have done the same thing but, being a woman, those words naturally came out of my mouth.

I grabbed my brownish-green baby and was ready to throw him in the shower with me when I realized his um-bilical cord hadn't come off yet so I couldn't get him com-pletely WET. AAHH!! I just screamed, which is what my brownish-green baby began to do. So I kind of propped him up on the side of the sink with just his feet hanging in and washclothed him off. But the poop just kept smear-ing. To make matters even worse, it was getting all over me, so every time my baby would lean back into me he got poop all over him again. There was an endless cycle of poop. Finally, with my husband's help, my son was pink again and Charlie the charcoal nub was still intact.

My friends and I named this process "shitting up the back," which caught on in my house as my husband shouted out at 3:00 A.M. yet again. Our brownish-green baby was back. But this time we were prepared. Instead of pulling the outfit off over his head, we simply cut it off using rounded-edge scissors (rounded so you can't hurt the baby). We did it!! And this time we didn't have to dig crap out of our baby's nostrils, which did make the cleanup a tad easier.

Between runny baby poo and diapers that just don't fit, no matter what, it's almost impossible to believe that you're not going to have to go through a similar experience in your baby's early months. That month we had to throw away at least twenty-five good outfits. Speaking of outfits, you will find yourself changing your baby's outfit at least four to five times a day. Between spit-ups and diaper leakage, there's just no way around it.

It's when your baby starts to eat more solid food that things become bizarre. I remember changing a diaper and shouting, "Ew, he just pooped like a human." Meaning his poo was in a log, ya know, like our grown-up poo. It kind of freaked me out. I almost preferred the runny poo. To wipe up after a log just seemed weird. Until, of course, I changed my 1,000th log-poop diaper. I kinda got used to it.

By the "human poo" stage, you get to experience all different kinds of adventures. I was watching my son play with his toys while taking a bath. He was pointing to the duckie, and he said, "Cow."

I was so happy just to hear him say "cow" that I congratulated him. Then he pointed to the next thing and said, "Cow."

I said, "No, baby, that's a leaf . . ."

"Weef . . ."

"No, baby, it's a leaf. How did that get in the tub?"

I bent over to grab the leaf and realized quickly that it was a poo log, NOT A LEAF!!!! I screamed in horror because my boy was sitting in a tub with his poo floating around him. He totally crapped in the tub. I quickly pulled him out and threw him in the shower. That was the day my son learned to say poo-poo . . . just a little too late.

Even though it might gross or weird you out, baby poo stories really are the best. For some reason people love sharing them. Just remember to be prepared for ANYTHING. Always pack a second change of clothes for your baby, no matter where you go. That one-foot turd could be your baby. I ain't shittin' ya!

Sex? . . . Yeah, Right!
Go Poke a Light Socket!

(Still Not in the Mood)

I f I heard the word sex mentioned in our house I ran into the bathroom, locked the door, plugged my ears, and started yelling "LALALALALALALALA" to get the thought out of my head. There was no way, no how, I was planning on having sex until I was ready. There was no mercy sex or even blow jobs going on in my household at all. At this point I thought porn was the best thing ever invented. I would much rather have my husband go watch a video than come within ten feet of me. This had nothing to do with not being attracted to him. He's a naughty-looking surfer boy, and I love riding any wave he's got when I'M ready!!! But I had no idea that being "healed" enough to have sex and actually wanting to have sex were two completely different things.

The one thing your doctor will tell you and your husband after delivery is to refrain from sex for about six weeks. I think all husbands roll their eyes, and most women want to say, "That's all? But I blew out my vagina and I can't even sit comfortably. You think in six weeks I'm gonna let him bang around in there? You're nuts."

What I say to that is, "YOU'RE RIGHT." To me, six weeks was so *not* the thing I wanted to hear. So I made sure I told my doc ahead of time to tell my husband at least three months. My doctor wanted my future business, so he did word it to say that "in Jenny's case," it would be good to wait about three months. AHH!! Thanks, Doc!

I did feel sorry for my husband at times. He had a glaze over his face, and developed carpal tunnel syndrome in his wrist from overworking it. Not that you care, but I made up for it later. MUCH MUCH later.

Besides waiting to heal physically, I feel like there are two other factors before you're ready: psychological and hormonal. These are my own theories, but to me they make sense. Psychologically, knowing how big your vagina got and having to squeeze a watermelon through it can kind of f*ck you up in the head. Especially if you tore and had stitches down there. In your head it just seems CRAZY to poke a penis in there even though you're "healed." At least in my head it didn't seem like enough time. Then you wonder if it's going to be a gaping hole or a cave, just like my husband's fear of throwing a hot dog down a hallway. So even though the doc says everything's all right "downstairs," it's the "upstairs" part that wasn't allowing me to move on.

Once you get past the psychological part of it all, you still go through the hormonal part. That's all your husband wants to hear, right? "My canooter doesn't hurt anymore and I'm not freaked out by your penis in there, but I just don't FEEL like having sex."

My mom has a great story of how, six months after having given birth, she and my dad were having sex (ew, gross) and she would tell him it STILL hurt. So she went back to the gyno and told him she thought he stitched her almost shut. The doc took a look down there and smiled. I think my mom still had enough room to land a 747, but she was so tense during sex from not wanting it that it made her feel like her canooter was sewn shut.

I remember feeling the same thing about five months after delivery when everything was supposed to be back to normal and we started having sex again. Something was wrong. Not just being exhausted from sleepless nights or endless poopie diapers. Sex was very different. I couldn't have an orgasm for months, and I felt like the Mojave Desert. My husband was starting to think it was him. I assured him it wasn't. I didn't know what to do and I started worrying, *Am I gonna be orgasmless forever?* That would totally suck. I would have to give up comedy and do dramas from now on because I would be pissed off all the time.

Then I saw one of those ads on TV showing women in menopause who lost their sex drive and found out they were lacking testosterone and used some sort of a patch that gave them a testosterone boost. I figured that HAD to be it. Maybe the medical industry didn't know that women who gave birth were also lacking testosterone and could use the patch. Childbirth must have sucked all of my testosterone out of my body. That had to be it!! So, I went to my gyno and told him I wanted a testosterone patch. He looked at me strangely for a beat and smiled. "Why?" he asked.

So I told him my problems, and he said that lacking testosterone was most likely not the cause, and I assured him he was wrong and I was right. I had to be right. I wanted a medical explanation for why I was feeling anti-sexual after so many months. The sad thing was he COULDN'T give me one. He told me to try some porn.

UGH! No more porn!! I want to feel stimulated on my own, not from watching a creepy guy hump a skanky Barbie in order to get off. So I left, testosterone patch-LESS!!

Then a wise woman said to me it takes nine months to build up your pregger hormones and nine months for them to go down. I also heard that same saying in regards to my fat ass. But it was the only hope I had, and it seemed true in my case. It took at least eight months and a getaway trip with my husband to Vegas to kickstart my engine. I felt good, like a woman again. I was so grateful that my husband was so patient with me. It's so important to communicate with your husband and let him know that it's not him. So, now you know that if it takes a long time for you to get it ON, don't worry cuz if this horndog eventually found delight in a boner, you will too. *RUFF RUFF!*

The Million-Dollar Manicure

(Cutting the Baby's Nails)

I've always been told by my short list of ex-boyfriends that I have the ugliest hands they had ever seen. I didn't believe the first guy, but when the fourth guy told me in the same polite tone I started to believe them. For most of my life I've been a tomboy, and so I never cared about my nails, until my choice of occupation forced me to endure acrylics here and there. To this day, I still hate maintaining my nails, but when I don't, that's all I can stare at when I watch myself on TV. "Look at those man-hands. I look like I'm about to go chop some wood using my bare man-hands."

Anyway, when my son was born, I looked down at his hands and noticed that he was blessed with Mommy's hands. Thank God he was a boy. When he gets a little older one day I can show him what his hands are going to look like as a grown-up. "Hey, Evan, look how strong and masculine and even hairy your hands are gonna be." I'm sure he'll be proud.

Within a few days of coming home from the hospital, I noticed that my son had some scratches on his face. I hadn't introduced him to the dogs yet so I knew it didn't come from them. Then one day I caught him in the act. He had some bad gas pains that made him cry, and he clenched up and dug his nails into his cheek. He didn't know that he was the one doing it so he wouldn't let up on his grip. I had to pull him off of himself. I grabbed his "mini-mommy" hand and looked at his nails. They were longer than any Beverly Hills bimbo's I had ever seen. I didn't realize that these suckers grew so fast, but I guess when all you're eating is milk, you're gonna grow some long chick nails.

I got out the baby nail clippers and took his "mini-mommy" hand in mine and slowly brought the clippers close to his finger. Sweat started dripping down my face out of complete fear of hurting my baby or possibly removing a finger. So, I took a breath and kind of walked around the house. My heart was beating fast because I was THAT scared. So I threw a few shadow punches in the air and started singing the *Rocky III* anthem, "Eye of the Tiger." I was determined!

Once again, I grabbed his little finger and brought the clippers in close. There was no oxygen entering my body because I couldn't breathe at all now. I didn't want to make a wrong move. To me, this was like surgery. I slid the clippers under the nail and started sweating again. So I stopped and got up and started yelling at myself. I felt so stupid.

I knew every new mom had to go through this, but I wondered if anyone got as freaked out as I did. I looked at my boy and tried to figure out an alternative. I thought I remembered hearing about some moms biting their kids' nails off. Sounded strange, but I didn't care. I thought my own choppers might be better then metal ones. So I stuck his finger in my mouth but it was too tiny to locate the nail with my teeth. I was so frustrated with myself that I did the only thing I could do at that moment. I put two socks over his hands and called it a day.

And I gotta tell ya, I kind of gloated on and on about how creative I was. I mean, I really thought I was onto something for a second. I thought for sure no one had thought of this invention and I was *sooo* imagining myself selling it on the Home Shopping Network and becoming stupid rich, like J-Lo rich. I even called my mom and told her, and she said, "Honey, they sell baby mittens in stores just for that reason, so babies don't scratch themselves."

Damn it! Somebody got there first!

But my mom also told me that I couldn't just throw socks on my son and walk away. I still had to cut his nails and then I could put something over his hands. Ugh! So I waited for Daddy to come home from a trip and had him do it. He also had sweat dripping down his face trying to perform this crazy procedure. Needless to say, I ran out and got those mittens so we could maybe get away with not cutting them for a while.

Then my friend came over and pulled off my son's mittens and screamed in horror. My baby was now a few weeks older and had Count Dracula nails. They were so long they almost curled. I played dumb. "Oh, wow, they must have grown overnight. I feel like my husband just clipped them yesterday." (Yeah, right, like a month ago.)

So I was forced to grab the clippers and cut them. I dug in deep and put the clippers right up to his nail and clipped. Something was off because the next thing I heard and saw was my baby screaming and blood coming down his finger. I KNEW IT!!!!!!! I KNEW I COULDN'T DO IT!! I picked up my baby and started crying with him. I didn't know what to do or how to apologize for Mommy sucking at nail cutting. I should have just let him grow old with mittens on.

It kills me right now to tell you that my son has gotten cut more than once. My husband did it, and then I asked my girlfriend to come over and clip his nails and she cut him—it was crazy. I left those mittens on my son for like three months. Finally my mother-in-law came in for a visit and said, "I think at this age he's supposed to discover his hands and learn how to control them."

Shit! She was right. The mittens finally had to come off.

If you're at all like I am and just horrified of cutting your baby's nails, ask your pediatrician to "show you how" during your visit. Then just keep asking him how to do it until he catches on. With Evan, I always forgot because they were covered by his mittens (which are really a great thing if you don't abuse them like I did). I still wish I had invented those damn things first.

A New Mom's BIGGEST Fear

(Crib Death)

This is one of the initial fears you will experience as a new mom that will carry on throughout your first year. Every new mom talks about it, and I'm glad they do. The good news is that crib death, otherwise known as SIDS, is way down, but it haunts all moms at night as they lay their little birds to sleep.

The "old" way of having babies sleep was on their tummies. And by old I mean all the way back around

1994. 1994? Wow, that's like when Britney Spears was actually still a virgin. Anyway, I guess back then they figured babies wouldn't choke if they spit their milk up in
the middle of the night. Then they did a study and found
that fewer babies died from crib death when they slept on
their backs. And that was that.

Now, when you see the nursery in the hospital, all the
babies are on their backs or sometimes on a slant. When
I say slant, I mean on a slant cushion or with a blanket
tucked along the side of the baby's back so if he spits up
it will slide down the side of his face. I highly recommend
using the "slant" method. Just remember to rotate the
baby so he doesn't develop a slanted head. One night
slant to the right, then the next night slant to the left. That
way you'll have a safer baby with a pretty-shaped head.
Also, experts suggest not using a blanket to lightly cover
your baby. Instead, wrap up the baby like a burrito, just
like they do in the hospital. Once he grows out of the
burrito-wrapping age, just dress him in warm PJs.

The first night home I was terrified. Just imagining
anything happening to my bird crushed my insides. The
grim reaper of newborns was out there, and I wanted to
dice him up in my blender and feed him to my neighbor's
barking dog. I was going to make sure the bastard never
got near my kid, even if that meant waking up every hour
to check on him, which was exactly what I did in the be-

ginning. I had a twin bed set up in his room, which is where I slept for about two months. I wanted my son to get used to his crib and not become dependent on sleeping in my room, so I joined him in his. I loved staring at him and listening to those inhales and exhales while I fell asleep. Who needs ocean waves crashing or a stream of water to relax you when you've got baby breaths? If I could have bottled them up I would have.

So, the first night I got up about every hour to check my son's breathing. I didn't set an alarm; I had the old Mommy clock now inside me that told me to wake up every hour. As days passed and I felt a little bit more comfortable, I relied on his feeding-time wake-ups, which were about every three hours. If he ever went past three hours without waking up for food, my body would bolt up and I would check on him. I know this sounds crazy but it's just a new mom thing. I'm sure Baby #2 won't get as much obsessed attention.

Anyway, to continue about my paranoia, sometimes when the baby would sleep deeply and I didn't hear any breathing, I would run over to him and kind of softly poke him until he made a noise. Unfortunately, the noise was usually "WAA WAA" because I accidentally woke him up. But I didn't really mind. Hey, if he was crying, that meant he was breathing!

Some women I've spoken to say that they sleep with

their newborns in their own beds. I would be so terrified of rolling over my baby or smothering him with my blanket that I never would have tried that. I can't tell you how many times I've slept with my little dog and accidentally shucked him right off the bed.

The good news for all of you, though, is that since my son was born, they now have baby monitors with alarms set on them to go off if the baby stops breathing. I love technology. If you feel that you might be as paranoid as I am, then I highly suggest getting one to put your mind at ease. I know I'm getting one for the next baby. Did I just say next baby? Boy, all this baby talk is making me crave another baby.

Anyway, if you want to kick the "grim reaper of the baby world" right in the balls, get one of these monitors and follow the new rules when it comes to sleeping requirements. It's worth it!

Hey, Girlfriend . . . Hello? . . . What Happened to All My Girlfriends?

(Changing of the Guard)

Thank God for girlfriends! How could you live without them? They're the first people I call after I'm done watching some skanky reality show to dish about all the sluts making out with whomever. I love it. And, of course, those wild nights out—I have a few classic memories of us staggering down Sunset Boulevard and peeing in somebody's alley. I thought for sure my friendly chickpack would always be united and friends till the end.

Even though some of us eventually got married, we still remained close. In fact, the married ones would live vicariously through the single ones. We'd listen to stories about some new boyfriend's crooked penis and love it!! But once you have a baby, things dramatically change.

Let me start by telling you this . . . once you become a mom, anyone who is still single in your life will think you are the most boring person to talk to. You might not know this because she will fake you out by smiling and nodding, but she doesn't honestly give a shit about your baby's new tooth. What she's really doing is thinking about how she's going to get her purse back from the hairy, creepy guy she slept with last night.

So you slowly stop getting as many calls from your single friends, and then you start to notice yourself talking every day to your friends who have babies. It's really bizarre to watch it happen because you thought your clique was unbreakable. But you're not there anymore when your girlfriend calls drunk from a bar at 3:00 A.M. with a booty-call guy shouting in the background. Nor do you want anything to do with that anymore. You'd rather clean up your baby's puke than your girlfriend's. So you make the sad transition of moving on from your wild friends and growing closer to the ones who just bought really cute diaper bags.

This is also another time in your life when you will

become friends with people you don't really want to become friends with just because they're mommies. If you make a regular schedule of going to the park with your baby, you will find yourself bumping into the same mommies. This can be great when you meet some new cool ones to join your mommy circle, but when you come across a mommy stalker, just be careful. She's the one who wants to plan "playdates" at your house while her baby is sucking on a Jim Beam pacifier.

So, just know that the whole changing of girlfriends thing is kind of normal. It happens to all of us, and I can tell you that the new mommies I've met who have joined my mommy circle far outweigh the drunken girlfriends who can't remember what bar they left their underwear in. . . .

You'll see!

What's Up, Doc?

(Endless Visits)

Taking your son to the pediatrician for his weekly and monthly checkups is good for one thing— forcing you to put on deodorant and get out of the house. And if you got lucky and picked a cute pediatrician, you might add lip gloss and mascara to that routine. Other than that, going to the doctor was truly a pain in the ass, at least for me.

By the time we arrived at the doctor's office for my

son's first weekly checkup, he had already puked on himself in the car. Because I didn't want to look like a mom who couldn't keep her kid clean, I changed him in the parking lot. By the time we got into the elevator, he had shit through his pants. So I used the restroom in the lobby and changed his outfit again. By the time the doctor called us in, he was out of outfits. I did have an emergency outfit I kept in the trunk of my car, but it was one of those outfits that Aunt Martha gave him that had elephants with wings flying through rainbows. Need I say more about why it's in the trunk as an emergency outfit? Luck was on my side for once and there was no need for it . . . yet.

The first checkup was exciting. The doc made sure that God had screwed everything on okay. No missing bolts. He gave me the baby's height and weight on a piece of paper that said "one week," and I couldn't wait to run home and put it into his scrapbook. The first month you will probably take your baby once a week. That will move to twice a month, then once a month.

The hard part for me was watching my boy get shots. That needle would poke into that tiny butt cheek, and it killed me. It was crazy, throughout the course of the first year, just how many shots my son had to have. I couldn't believe it. I was scared knowing that there are still so many diseases out there that he needed protection from.

Every visit had one or two shots. No wonder my son screamed when we walked in the office door.

In that first month home you are going to find that putting your pediatrician on your speed dial is a great idea. My husband and I called him almost every day that month. The first week my son had bad red bumps on his face. We called the doc and he said it was acne. The next day there were blisters on his lips. I called the doc and he said it was due to him sucking on the nipple so hard and that it was normal. Then we called him up about my son's screaming with gas pains, and he said that was normal too. I wondered if it was normal for me to be calling every day, and the answer is yes. Most pediatricians see a new parent coming a mile away, and expect endless phone calls in the beginning. I sure did live up to his expectations.

You should also know that sometimes you need to take matters into your own hands. I am a firm believer in "Mommy knows best." If you call your doc and he says just to give the baby Tylenol, but you think it could be something worse, DO SOMETHING ABOUT IT! Just because a new mom cries wolf a lot doesn't mean her instincts are wrong. Moms have the best internal radar, and their own instincts can outdo Superman's any day of the week.

My own son's gas pains became so bad I would cry

with him. Even though my doc told me they were pretty normal, I just had to do something. The gas pains were causing his little veins to pop out, and he was so constipated that when he finally went poo-poo there was blood in his stool. I continued to bug his pediatrician. He told me to start giving him some water to help ease the constipation. I told him I wanted to try switching his formula. The doc still wanted me to wait it out, but I didn't. Mommy radar was on, so I put on my cape and flew to the store and bought different formula. It worked. I was so happy.

So, let's review. Bring numerous extra outfits to every visit, ask questions, don't be afraid to call, and, most important, keep mommy radar on at all times!!! And if your doc is really cute, go ahead and put the nicer sweatpants on.

Thank God for Baby Einstein

(Baby Rotation)

Even though you love your baby more than words can say, you will at times look at him or her and think, "You're just a blob!!" These little precious beings are so beautiful, yet at the same time . . . kind of boring during the newborn stage. They don't really respond to you, and sometimes you feel like you want a little gratitude for all the hard work you're doing, and all you get are crap-filled diapers. But you adore your child, nonetheless.

I remember trying to figure out how to entertain my son. He got to the age when he was still a blob and couldn't sit up yet but wanted to be stimulated constantly. So I bought him a mobile that you put on the floor with little shapes that hang down. He would bat his little hands around at them and look all bug-eyed, like he was invited to the best party in town. That was such a lifesaver. Unfortunately, his "fun" lasted only long enough for me to throw a load of laundry in and make my bed. Then he wanted more. So I would play with him for a bit and then I would put him in his swing. After that was maxed out, I would take him for a walk. Then, in order to get more things done around the house, I would throw on a Baby Einstein video and after that try to read him a colorful book, which he seemed to not really care about, and finally I would give him a bath and then put him to bed.

This rotation and this same schedule can drive a mom nuts. When it's the same thing every day, you tend to lose your mind. When all you can hum are the dumb jingles from your baby's video, it's time to figure out new things to add to your baby "rotation" schedule. I call it "rotation" because, during this "blob" phase, you really find yourself going from one thing to the next as far as things that can stimulate him or her without you having to do them all day long. I remember feeling guilty at times because he'd watch three back-to-back Baby Einstein videos, and I don't think he was even able to see the TV yet. But some-one has to make dinner and then clean it up so you resort to your rotation objects to kind of babysit for you. My girlfriends would all talk on the phone and say, "Okay, time to move my blob to the swing," or "Okay, time to move the blob to the bouncy." It's physically impossible to be the sole entertainer during this phase. I do think it's very important when he starts to get a little older, but as long as you're doing your fair share, I think that's good.

The one great thing about this age, though, is that you can take your baby blob just about everywhere. Because they mostly sleep and don't try to sit up yet, they're pretty cozy staying in their little carrying seat while you enjoy a nice dinner out. And for some reason they can shut out loud ambient noise and still take a snooze. I highly sug-gest doing as much as you can outdoors during this phase because baby blob sits up before you know it.

When I would talk to my mom during the blob months, I would tell her how hard it was not getting a re-action from my son after spoiling him with endless amounts of love. I would snuggle with him, give him tons of kisses, and sing to him—nothing. I knew he was too young to be like, "Hey, thanks, lady," but it was still kind of disheartening. Then my mom told me something that will stay with me forever, which a dear old friend once told her: "Jenny, everything responds to love."

I was quiet for a moment and really thought that through. It's true! Love is so powerful that, even though the energy can't physically be seen, it affects everything it touches. I knew that my baby was responding to my love in his own way. He knew that when I held him he could stop crying because my love was there for him. That was his way of saying, "Because you love me the way you do, I don't need to feel scared. Thanks, Mom." From that point on, I never doubted it again.

So even though your blob can't high-five you or pat you on the back, know that your love shines through, creating the special person you want your blob to become.

Finding Mrs. Doubtfire

(The Search for the Perfect Babysitter)

Hollywood's version of a full-time nanny is not just one who comes in while you are at work. "Full time" means having a "day" nanny and a "night" nurse, on top of their assistants. I had none of the above. But I know there are plenty of women out there who work full time and have to get help. And for those who don't, you still need the occasional babysitter so you can do tasks here and there or go to weddings or even have a rare "date night" with your husband.

Back in the old days, when my mom needed someone to babysit, she would ask the sixteen-year-old girl living a few houses down to come over and watch us. Out in L.A., that's just not possible. It's such a bizarre, inbred city of people from across the country, who are all out here to fulfill their dream—and those dreams might be stalking Pamela Anderson. You just don't know who your neighbors are. And most people in Hollywood will tell you that you don't talk to your neighbors.

That said, I was desperately seeking a sitter who I could count on and trust. The first thing I did—and you probably will to—is exhaust all my siblings and relatives to the point of them being tapped out. When my sisters would pop in for a visit, I would grab my car keys and bolt out the door saying, "I just need to run to the grocery store." That's usually how I got my grocery shopping done. But when people start to catch on, you're screwed. You're left standing at the front window, staring out at the curb, hoping to see a familiar car pull up. Those "pop-in" visits will seriously dwindle.

So, you're left to officially start your search. I started by asking around and received my first recommendation through a friend. She told me that her nanny's friend was looking for some part-time work and, since her own nanny came from good stock, I should be really pleased. She told me that the nanny's friend was a little Chinese woman with a sweet demeanor. I gave her recommendation the benefit of the doubt and I set up an interview.

That day came, and as my husband and I waited anxiously on the porch, we talked about our fears of having a stranger in our home to watch the most important thing in our lives, our son. We wanted to know that whomever we chose was going to see the traits in our baby that we love and adore and spoil him with affection.

A car pulled up, and two cute little Chinese women stepped out. My husband and I looked at each other and kind of smirked. We thought it was funny that the sitter brought a friend with her but figured maybe they were going out after the interview or something. So they approached, and we introduced ourselves. Ming was the one we were interviewing, and her friend was Kim. I invited them in and we sat down. They both looked really sweet, like Chinese grandmas, and I hoped they were going to impress me with their great stories. My first question was to Ming. "Tell me about yourself and how long you've been watching babies." I thought that was a pretty good opener. Not necessarily an icebreaker but I wanted to get to the point.

I smiled and waited for a response. Ming smiled back and looked at Kim. Then Kim leaned toward her and said,

"*Sin chow kin sa be koe low cjhow.*" Ming responded with, "*Tao kin la shiun bang lin.*" My husband grabbed my finger under the table so hard that I squeaked. As I'm sure you've figured out, Kim wasn't just a friend, she was translating for our potential babysitter!!!!

My husband and I were speechless. We just stared in awe as Kim told us Ming's response in broken English. "She-say-a-long-time." Now, mind you, Ming could very well make a great babysitter, but I really wanted someone to whom I could say, "Only give him one ounce of Tylenol today," and I don't think Kim was going to be her sidekick to translate every time. My husband and I didn't want to be rude, so we smiled a lot and gave them a good twenty minutes before we ended the interview.

I had a hard time wanting to interview anyone else. I just stayed home a lot. If you didn't see me on TV for a while, this is where I was—on the sofa with my baby, watching *Oprah*. Then I started to get calls again from my agent, urging me to get back to doing some guest spots or something so I didn't end up on a "whatever-happened-to-her" list. I didn't really care, to tell ya the truth. I was really happy just being a mom, but knowing how much private schools were in L.A. I had to get a-crackin'. I got lucky because my sister was between jobs at the time so I paid her to help me out here and there.

Then I was offered a couple of guest spots and knew I

needed more help than usual for a couple of weeks. Once again I asked around and heard about a girl who was moving to L.A. and was looking for a nanny job because she was leaving a "rock star celebrity family" she worked with for five years. Great!

So, she came over and seemed very sweet. She was a little nerdy but I didn't think that mattered—although, now that I think back, that should have been my first clue. I told her I would give her a couple of tries. The first time I came home from work, everything seemed to be fine. She told me stories about the cute things my son did that day, which I loved hearing. The next time I came home I found her crying because the guy she moved down to L.A. for broke up with her and she was in pieces. I felt bad for her, but all I could think about was my own baby sitting in the same spot all day while she was crying to her boyfriend on the phone. Things were going south for this girl, but I hung in there and gave her another shot.

Finally I came home from work one day and asked her how things had gone. "Evan really likes the taste of mud!" she said.

I blinked hard and shouted in my head, "Um—what did you just say, bitch? *Evan really likes the taste of mud?*" But I was able to respond with, "What do you mean?"

She replied, "Well, by the time I got to him he was chewing it and smiling."

WHAT???? Okay, let's just examine the first part of that sentence, "By the time I got to him . . ." She was obviously not even near him. Follow that up with, "He was chewing it and smiling!!" Oh, my GOD! Needless to say, I fired her.

A few months later, I was talking to my sister about her acting class. She was telling me how she'd met a bunch of girls just "off the bus" from Indiana, Ohio, Texas, and everywhere in between—young sweet girls who'd moved to this horrible town, looking for fame and stardom but inquiring about some part-time babysitting because that's all they did back home. That was perfect for me. I met a few of them and fell in love. They were good eggs. Young, sweet, and they loved kids. To this day I still use them, and they rotate between whatever small gigs they get. I still have yet to get a full-time person. But I know that's inevitable when I start really working again.

I never called a nanny service, for some reason. I always relied on word of mouth, which, as you can see, doesn't always work. If you live in a good town and are looking for a weekend babysitter, I highly recommend putting up an ad on your local high school bulletin board. I would always check that out in high school and I was a DAMN good babysitter. Also, there are a lot of children's play gyms opening up around the country. The girls who work there always offer their services and know a bunch of songs and games for your child.

So, just be smart, ladies. If you're a mom who needs full-time help, do your homework and get a background check and possibly a nanny cam. Let them know it's there if you want to, but I just think it's better to be safe than sorry. Unless, of course, you think mud is one of the five major food groups. I personally don't.

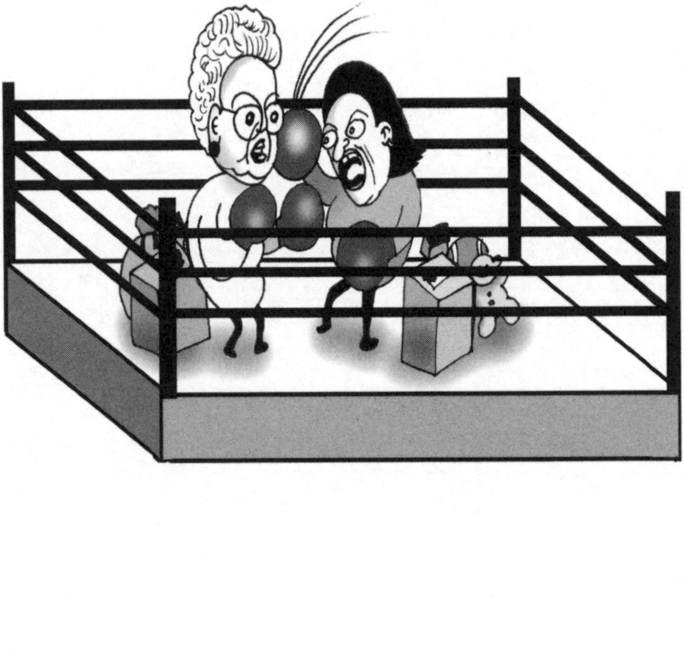

In This Corner We Have Grandma, and in This Corner We Have Grandma

(Helpers or Villains?)

I t's most likely going to happen to us someday. Our children will be raised, we'll watch them get married to someone we don't like, and then they'll have children and we'll become grandmothers. Kind of freaks me out when I think about it. At least grannies are looking better and better these days. The exception of course being Joan Rivers. Then again, she looks pretty good for being 170.

I had both of my mothers in the delivery room with me. I love them both so much I wanted them to share in the "beauty" of my delivery. Each mother was holding one of my fifty-pound legs. Needless to say, they had VIP seats. My mom felt like my guardian angel, making sure no doctors were doing anything wrong. My mother-in-law always makes me laugh, so I knew I could count on her for a good one when things got tough for me. And she came through when I was squeezing hard, by shouting out in her high-pitched, Minnie Mouse voice, "WOW, it looks like a raspberry tart down there." I couldn't help but laugh at that visual.

I also thought having my two moms there for the birth might make them feel more connected to my son. Maybe they would spoil him with love even more. They didn't get to actually see my son being born, though, because I had the emergency C-section. But that didn't matter. They still spoil him more than I ever could have imagined.

It was so sweet watching my mom hold my son for the first time. I knew what it felt like to be in her arms, so I knew he was in good hands. It was amazing to watch them together and to see a new generation begin. I was her baby all these years, and now she was holding mine. Goose bumps, ya know?

Nowadays, there are so many divorces and remarriages within all of our family circles that our kids could possibly have up to, like, four grandmas. That's when you start making up nicknames for each grandma so your kid can differentiate who's who. Like, "We're going to see Piano Grandma today," or, "Do you want to sleep over with the grandma who stole Grandpa away from Piano Grandma after thirty years of cleaning up his shit?" That one might be too long for your kid, but you get the idea.

I've been blessed with mine but I hear GREAT stories about other grandmas—full-out competitor grandmas who try to outdo each other. My girlfriend wants to pull out her hair over hers. My advice to her was to give them some canes and let them battle it out on the back lawn. I'm sure that would sell a few million videos, *BACKYARD WRESTLING GRANDMAS: They Might Be Old, But Their Dentures Are Young.*

You might notice yours lecturing on how to do certain things. If this bothers you in the least bit, I highly suggest letting your mother or mother-in-law know that you really want to try the whole mothering thing out on your own. If you don't set boundaries right from the start I promise it will only get more difficult as time goes on. They really are just trying to be helpful, but what they need to know is that things have changed since they gave birth. We have microwaves now, so no need to boil the bottle. We have disposable diapers. Brandy for teething isn't really "the thing" anymore. So find a comfortable way of letting them know that you really want to try to figure things out on your own. Whatever ya do, don't piss them off. They still make the BEST babysitters.

You should have fun watching your husband deal with your mom when she comes for a sleepover visit. My husband loved it, of course, because he got to sleep in. But others aren't so lucky. You've all seen the cartoons that show a mother-in-law sleeping over and the husband is staying out in a tent on the front lawn. Wait till you hear a grandma tell a husband, "Don't hold his head like that," or, "Make sure you clean all the poo-poo hiding under his testicles. You should know—you have them, don't you?" Mind you, you may have heard similar things from his mom, so now he can see how it feels. But you know the visit must end when your husband starts singing *"Grandma got run over by a reindeer..."*

We can't be too hard on them, remember. Having your own baby now gives you so much more appreciation for how they did it without microwaves and disposable diapers. My mom raised four girls, each two years apart, without much money, and managed to give us so much love, a strong sense of self, and support, no matter how bad Jenny was that week. I can only hope I am able to step into her shoes and do the same for my son. What a perfect mom I would be. P.S. Mom, I was the one who wrote on the couch with markers when I was seven and blamed it on Amy. It's been driving me crazy. I thought it was time to come clean.

The WWE Baby Champion of the World!

(Daddy Playtime)

I'm sure most of you had dolls you used to play with when you were little. And I'm sure some of you weren't as gentle as you pretended to be. I would cut off all my dolls' hair and use marker to put makeup on their eyes. I was definitely one of these girls who manhandled their dollies. When my mom found a doll head in the oven, she knew it had to be Jenny's. With age and wisdom, I can assure you that I've outgrown this, but I think husbands still need to be taught that newborns are not as strong as their GI Joe dolls.

When you're in the hospital and you gently pass your baby over to a nurse, you think they're going to take it to the nursery and care for it like it's the most expensive ceramic piece auctioned off at Sotheby's. Instead they toss babies around like fish in the Seattle fish market. Okay, that may be exaggerating a bit, but that's how it may seem. From the way they give babies their first bath to the way they burp them, nurses make it seem that babies are unbreakable, but they're not. These people are professionals. They should have shirts saying, "Don't try this at home." They know exactly how to hold the baby safely while quickly caring for his needs. We earthlings need to take it down a notch. I'm not saying to be terrified of handling your baby, just know your baby's limitations.

My husband didn't quite understand the concept of wobbly-head baby. I came home from the grocery store to find him tossing our two-week-old in the air. Needless to say, I screamed in horror and showed him that our son's neck was too weak for "airplane." Then next time I came home, I found him rolling on the ground with him wrestling. Once again, I freaked! He said they were bonding by doing some wrestling moves. I told him AGAIN that three-week-old babies can't really wrestle yet and that rocking him would be a great bonding experience. I think men get so bored with newborns that they honestly think that playing with them at this age is the right thing to do.

I would also catch my husband making the baby dance to music. At three weeks old my son was being forced to bounce around to Eminem. My husband would also put him on a skateboard and wheel him around the house. I broke out in rashes whenever I'd see him doing that. Then one day my husband walked in the door with a one-month-old birthday present. I thought that was so cute until he opened the bag and pulled out a football. I said, "What the hell are you thinking?"

Of course, I got the usual response from my husband, "Will you relax! It's gonna get him ready for the big game. He's gonna love it."

I've got to admit that it was cute seeing them "play," but at this age it's just not safe. So make sure you warn your hubby that babies are fragile and that if they need to try out some wrestling moves to do it on the dog because the baby is just too young and the dog will at least give him a good fight. And, hopefully a good bite in the ass!

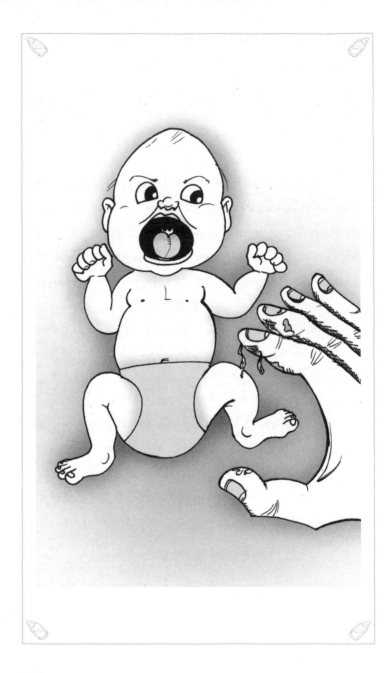

Hey, Honey, the Germs Are Over for Another Visit!

(Unwanted Visitors)

I t will absolutely BLOW your mind when you get the opportunity to meet the Germs for the first time. First of all, you will be immediately protective of your newborn at all times—making sure his diaper isn't too tight, making sure he's always breathing, making sure he doesn't roll off the changing table, and *yada-yada*. The one thing you don't think about is GERMS until visitors start flocking to your house. Now, mind you, I do not have obsessive-compulsive disorder. I do not wash my hands 700 times a day or avoid cracks on the sidewalk. In fact, I'm kind of sloppy. But I think every new parent starts feeling a bit germophobic when you're waiting for your bun to get out of the oven.

Before my baby even came home from the hospital, I planned on sanitizing everything in his room. It seemed logical, considering that dust built up in there while we were waiting for my little bun to be born. Then I saw this story on *Oprah* about dangerous products that could harm or kill your newborn. I was GLUED to the TV. The first story was about a mom who left a bottle of baby oil on the counter and her baby drank it and became seriously ill and died. So I ran into the bathroom and got rid of the baby oil. I'm not saying to do the same, just put it in a safe area with all your other hazardous things. The next story was about how Kelly Preston (John Travolta's wife) was preparing to bring home her new baby and sanitized the hell out of her nursery. Her baby became sick and she found out the fumes were the culprit. Boy, thank God for Oprah. I honestly believe she's some sort of a guardian angel for the human race.

So I took what I learned and did some light dusting. I was prepared. Well, not really. I wasn't expecting Mr. and Mrs. Stomach Flu to come over in the first two weeks to visit my baby. They were followed by Mr. Oh-I-Had-

Really-Bad-Diarrhea-All-Day asking, "Hey, is it my turn to hold the baby?!" It was truly UNBELIEVABLE. I know that people are excited to come see your creation, but for God's sake, have the brain cells to know that if you're squirting chocolate shakes out of your ass all day, don't come visit my baby!

You will also experience more friends, relatives, and sometimes strangers who come up to your baby and put their finger in the grip of your baby's hand. As most of you know, babies grab onto a finger tightly and we earthlings find it to be oh-so-cute. And it is totally cute when it's MY finger. Damn, I sound so bitchy right now, but this is the thing—babies are fragile in those first weeks. They haven't had a chance to build up an immune system yet. So, even if Aunt Martha comes over healthy as a nut and puts her finger in your baby's grip, who knows what's ON Aunt Martha's finger or where the hell Aunt Martha's finger's been? What orifice was she poking around in? Hopefully not Uncle Hank's. As soon as Aunt Martha removes her finger from the baby's grip, you can be damn sure the baby is putting his little hand right into his mouth. So then I panic because my baby probably just ate part of Uncle Hank's ass.

Okay, on to the next OH MY GOD scenario. People who put their own finger in your baby's mouth to gnaw on while the baby is teething. CAN YOU BELIEVE IT???????

Ahhh. That's when Psycho Mom completely busts a nut. All I remember was that my eyes crossed and my veins pulsed out of my head as I shouted, "WOW, I THINK THE BABY JUST POOPED," and snatched my baby back.

The sad part of the story is that it only gets worse. Playdates at your house; public parks loaded with children running around with green snot dripping down their faces, sneezing, coughing until you come home with pinkeye and lice. But by that time your baby's immune system has strengthened, so Junior should recover. You just have to remember to keep both of your hands as clean as you can and keep Mr. Hershey Squirts and Aunt Stinky Finger far away from your baby.

Say Cheeeeezy!!!

(Documenting Your Baby)

Yes, you are now a geeky parent who will be carrying around a camera *and* a video camera documenting your baby doing everything from blinking to smiling to eating his first green bean. We missed out on getting the first hospital photo. We were supposed to mail in money and fill out the order form. Screw that. We had no time. We were new parents, just trying to get by. Newborns always look like alien babies anyway. The hospitals really need to do something about their lighting. So we took documenting our son into our own hands.

The first few months we took picture after picture. I was so excited waiting for the film to come back. When I saw the pictures, it was kind of disappointing because they all looked the same. He was still just a blob. So, no matter where the picture was taken, he just lay there like his cute blob self. He was adorable, of course, but he couldn't do anything yet.

So I started dressing him up in funny outfits. I put him in a tuxedo when he was three weeks old. That was funny. Then I put Dad's shoes on him. That was pretty good. Then we needed to outdo ourselves, so my husband made a horror flick with my son as the lead actor and our dogs as supporting cast members. The movies continued, with the latest being my son sitting in his high chair holding some cards at a poker tournament.

When it came time to do my son's portraits, I knew I had to get the *cheeeeziest* money could buy—the reason being that moms in general are notorious for taking really cheesy pictures of their kids growing up, standing next to some fake plastic unicorn or something. So it had to be done! And where could you find the cheesiest of cheese portraits??? Sears, of course.

My baby needed some good, old-fashioned Sears portraits, and what made it even more exciting was the fact

that I had a coupon. I happily put him in a "tough boy" outfit and got a collection using a few different back-grounds. I gotta tell ya, your blob does look pretty damn cute with fake clouds behind him.

Then I moved it up a notch and had a life-size cutout made of him sitting on a surfboard. I loved it. I loved every stupid minute of myself being a total dork. I can't wait for my son's first day of school. I might get a film crew and hire some extras.

So don't forget to keep that battery charged and film in that camera. Looking back at the photos of your baby growing up will make you feel so good and so old all at the same time.

Can Someone Come Over to Do the Laundry and Clean the Toilet So I Can Take a Shower and Shave My Armpits Once This Week?

(Mommy Time)

My baby was about two months old when I looked down and saw my leg sticking out of my sweatpants. I was horrified! I was as hairy as Robin Williams. I couldn't believe it. Then I glanced quickly into the mirror and noticed that my overgrown roots were making me look like a hippie who stopped following the Grateful

Dead after twenty years. Then I brushed my fingers across my upper lip and realized that I hadn't waxed it and probably would be able to braid it soon. I didn't even dare check under my arms. I could tell that they were cushioned by something, and I took a good guess at what it was.

The damage was done. I looked like Bigfoot's bitch and felt like someone had to rescue me from the downward spiral of becoming a he-she. I could hear people on the street now . . . "Hey, is that Jenny McCarthy?" "No," someone would reply, "that's got to be her brother."

Becoming a new mom, you surrender all of your needs for the well-being of your baby. You are constantly on alert, making sure your energy is directed toward your baby instead of keeping up on the latest fashions. The problem is that you become so consumed by your baby's needs that you forget about your own. After a while, it can kind of make you feel like shit. The bigger problem is you have no time to do anything about it.

I remember someone saying when you put your baby down, take a nap or take a shower, but there still wasn't time to do that. I was doing laundry because the baby would go through an entire wardrobe in a day or I was making dinner or I was cleaning. I remember calling up my sister, begging her to come over so I could shower at least once that week. My shirt was sticking to me from all the baby spit-up.

The days I couldn't get anyone to come over, I would put my baby in his bouncy on the floor and drag him into the bathroom while I showered. It was the only way sometimes. Because your time is always the baby's time. I couldn't even go #2 without having to have him join me. Poor guy. No wonder he still cries when he walks into the bathroom.

Anyway, it got to the point where I couldn't handle becoming a hairy, five-foot puke rag for my baby. I needed some Mommy Time. So I forced myself to make a hair appointment and nail appointment. It's amazing that just getting a blow-dry can make you feel like a girl again and how cool a little nail polish can make you feel. I realized how important it was for a mommy to take the time to do SOMETHING for herself. It really does make us better mommies because we feel better about ourselves. This is a great time to start exercising if you can. It's one hour for you. When a week would pass with no Mommy Time, I would at least try to put makeup on that morning. It really does make you feel better, and your husband seems to enjoy it. You can't forget that you are also a wife, not just a new mom who looks like a hairy, five-foot puke rag for your baby.

So, just know that you are not alone when you look at your moustache in the mirror. There are many of us out there who feel your hairy pain. Just make sure you do something for yourself at least once a week, even if it is combing your legs.

Uh-Oh, My Baby Isn't Perfect

(Deformities)

Throughout your pregnancy you pray so hard that your child is born healthy. I'm sure you've heard stories or have seen medical TV shows showing mothers holding their sick or troubled babies and think, "God, I'll be a better person in life, just please give my child perfect health." I cry sometimes when I stop and think about those moms out there, trying to heal their sick children. I know every mother in the world would say, "Give us the pain, God! Just take it away from our sick babies."

Because of my son's insane delivery I was surprised that the only problems he suffered from were jaundice and a severe conehead. At least this is what I thought until people started asking me what was wrong with my son's head three months after delivery. His head shape was different than most kids' coneheads. It looked as if his skull plates (these are my terms) were crooked, causing his head to grow wide instead of round. At every doctor visit, the pediatrician would tell me to have him sleep on his side more, but he already was. The doctor was afraid that flattening was occurring. When your baby sleeps on one side all the time, a side of the head can flatten. That's why it is so important to rotate sides when your baby sleeps. I was already doing that and it wasn't changing things.

I knew my delivery screwed up my son's head, but I wasn't worried yet. I just thought that, with time, his head would round out. A few months later we could see that it was getting worse. The back of my son's head became severely flat, and the sides were starting to bulge out. My son's doc had me go see someone who specialized in "flat spots," and told us our son had one of the worst cases he had ever seen. Great! Thanks, doc—way to break the news to me nicely!

This doctor had treated so many kids with flat spots that he was going to try and use his technique to help my boy. He told me he had to make a cast molding of Evan's head and fit him with a custom helmet. Just the thought of him having to wear a helmet made me tear up. The doctor told me that I would have to keep it on him day and night. I said, "Well, can I at least take it off of him when I go to the grocery store? I don't want people staring at him like, *Oh, poor little baby.*"

He said, "Your baby won't know people are staring at him—just you."

I knew that. I just didn't want those sympathy eyes, ya know? I promised to keep the helmet on him. I would do anything. I was determined to make his head look better even if that meant growing his hair out to cover it. So what if my baby went to preschool looking like Fabio? It was better than the alternative.

The day they fitted his helmet, I cried. I was hoping he'd look like a motorcycle rider but he didn't. He looked like he was waiting for the short bus. I couldn't stand it, so I decided to get it spray-painted to look like a professional football helmet. I just had to decide which team color and logo I would go with. I'm from Chicago, so naturally I should have picked the Bears, but those colors don't really go with everything he might wear. (How girly is that?) The Raiders have silver and black. Those colors go great with everything. So that's what I went with. To all those Chicago fans out there, don't worry! He still wore his Chicago Bears PJs at night.

When the helmet came back from the artist, I cried again because it looked so good. I put it on my son and giggled. He looked so cute. Like a mini football player. From that point on, moms would stop me and ask where they could get a football helmet like that for their sons. I would politely tell them that they didn't want this one, for many reasons—the least being that it cost about $15,000 in therapy. The good news is that my son's head looks so much better now. The helmet didn't fix it completely—only about 80 percent, but hey, I'll take it. And if he becomes the new Fabio, you'll know why.

I know that this problem with my son doesn't compare to some people's, but I just want people to know that health should not be taken for granted. If and when your baby is born healthy, stop and give thanks because you are truly blessed. And to all those moms out there who suffer with their sick babies, my prayers are with you.

Burning the Muumuu!!

(Finally Losing the FAT)

The moment I knew that I finally had enough of my body was the day I begged God to put a zipper down the front of my torso so I could simply unzip myself and walk out of my fat suit. It was starting to disgust me. I was watching what I ate, but I wasn't really giving it the full-blown Hollywood try. The second most annoying thing besides your fat ass is how you don't fit into any clothes. I've heard women say that they wish there were a transitional clothing store because you don't fit into maternity and you don't fit into your old wardrobe. And the last thing you're going to do is spend money on clothes in sizes you don't plan on keeping. I took one last look at my housedress, otherwise known as my muumuu, and told myself to stop f*cking around and do something!

The next day, I hired a trainer and started doing an hour of cardio and weights three days a week. I was so determined that I kept chanting *Madonna, Madonna, Madonna* while I was on the treadmill. If Madonna was always so strong-willed, I could be too. A month went by, and I decided to reward myself with finally seeing how much I lost. I stepped on the scale and almost fell over. I'd lost NOTHING!! I bent down and banged the scale. It had to be wrong!! I'd been like a machine all month. I ate healthy and worked so hard. My trainer said it was because I was gaining muscle. UGH! Fine! But please explain why my cellulite still seemed to be dripping down my thighs and causing a rash between my legs where they rubbed together.

So I decided to lower my calories even more. I was down to sushi, salads, and vegetables every day. I did this for a month while continuing my strenuous exercise. I couldn't wait to weigh myself. At the end of that month I stepped my naked ass on the scale, and it said that I'd lost two pounds. TWO POUNDS!!!!!! This was bullshit!! I was doing everything I thought Madonna would be doing in my case, so what the hell? I was so upset that I told myself to do what most celebrities do. I was gonna starve myself. I couldn't take it anymore. Ten minutes later my stomach growled, and I ate. I could never be anorexic. I love food more than sex.

I then made an appointment to see my gyno. When he walked into the room, I broke down. I had a complete emotional tantrum in front of him while wearing that oh-so-flattering paper robe. He tried to calm me down. He went on to tell me that, based on his thirty-five-years of experience, it could take a woman three periods to finally start letting go of the fat. That our hormones almost hold onto it.

Three periods? I didn't get my first period until almost three months postdelivery. I still had one period to go. Ugh!! I figured he had to be right because I was doing everything possible to lose my fat suit. So I hit a drive-through McDonald's on the way home and cried my way through a Big Mac.

The next day I told myself to just shut up and be patient. I was still going to give losing weight a good effort, but I wasn't going to let it control my every thought. So I let go of my trainer and decided to join Weight Watchers.

(They are not paying me to say that, but I wish they would. I'm just being honest and letting you know that this really worked for me.) I went to the meetings with my baby, which they encourage you to do, and fell in love with the system. I was allowed to eat pizza while still dieting. I went every week and weighed in. I would even stand up at meetings and tell the women that Oreos talked to me in the grocery store aisle too. I was beginning to lose a steady three pounds a week. Because I was unmotivated to do anything cardio at the gym anymore, I bought a bike with a baby seat and went on bike rides. I also strollered my son everywhere. Those walks can really do wonders.

By the time of my son's first birthday, I was ten pounds away from my old weight. I was so happy my fat suit was almost gone.

I'm sure you've heard people say, "If you don't lose that pregnancy weight in that first year, you'll have the hardest time ever losing it." Well, I have a theory on why that is true. In that first year your child is eating pureed peas and liquid chicken, so you want nothing to do with his leftovers. But when your baby gets into the toddler years, he's having chicken nuggets and french fries and mac and cheese and YOU'RE FINISHING HIS FOOD!!! So you have that good window of gross baby food that won't tempt you. That's why I think they say, "Lose it the first year"—or temptation Happy Meals will get the best of you!

So, please know that weight loss does not happen overnight. If you're patient and at least make some effort along the way, you'll watch your ass shrink before your eyes. It just takes TIME! Even for Madonna!

My Baby's Smarter Than Your Baby . . . Oh, Yeah, Well, Your Baby's Ugly!

(Competitive Moms)

I know there's a little competitiveness inside all of us. I don't think I ever would have moved from the South Side of Chicago if I wasn't competitive. I always yearned to be the best at what I was doing, no matter what, even if that included being the beer-bong champion in college. I still have a hard time drinking beer ever since that event—but, hey, I won!

The first time I ever really noticed competitive moms

was way before I became pregnant. I was waiting at the deli counter to get some sliced ham and was totally eavesdropping on a conversation next to me. These two women just happened to run into each other while they were ordering their pound of whatever. The tone of their voices sounded so fake, I knew I had to listen in.

Soccer mom says, "Joey is getting so tall that his coach is thinking about moving him to varsity."

Basketball mom says, "Don't you think that puts more pressure on him, though? Trying to keep up with the varsity boys?"

Soccer mom: "Not at all. Joey is the captain of the team for a reason. He averages at least seven goals a game."

Basketball mom: "Well, my Tommy scores fifteen points a game, but I don't think I'd ever do that to him. They should develop with kids in their own age group."

Soccer mom: "But Joey's gifted. His coaches see huge potential in his future."

Basketball mom: "Well, so is Tommy. He got MVP this season."

Soccer mom: "MVP for his team or MVP for the ALL-STAR team? There's a big difference!"

Basketball mom kind of twitches and changes the topic. I wish there was a camera on my face as I watched them play "my son is better than your son." It was right out of a sitcom. I made a pact with myself never to be one of those moms. But I have sure met a few juicy ones along the way.

The moment your baby is born and you see him or her among all the other baby burritos in the hospital nursery, you will find yourself doing your first "comparison shopping." You first check and see if your baby looks pretty normal within the group—doesn't stick out in a crowd, if you know what I mean. No third leg or anything. I think this is pretty normal to do. But what about thoughts like, "Wow, thank God my baby's nose isn't ugly like that baby's nose?" Wrong type of comparison shopping!!

As your baby gets older you will find yourself continuing to "comparison shop" anytime you meet a baby the same age as your baby. Everybody does this, and it's completely obvious at any park. The scenario usually goes like this: I put my baby into a swing next to another baby who looks like it might be the same age. The other mommy says, "How old is your son?"

I reply, "Eight months," and she says, "Oh, mine too!"

We both smile, giggle, and then quietly stare down each other's baby, comparing his height, weight, and motor abilities.

This doesn't really let up throughout your child's first year. You'll pass a mom in the grocery store and smile at her baby, all the while doing a full head-to-toe exam. If you join any play-gyms or host any Mommy & Me's it can get out of control. And it's inevitable that you will encounter the annoying mommies who turn "comparison shopping" into "competitive shopping."

My first play-gym experience almost landed me in the police station because of a bad mommy. It started off with the usual "How old is your baby?"—which you know is fine, because I play that one too. But then came, "He's not crawling yet? Is something wrong with him?"

And like a defending mommy, I said, "No, some don't crawl until they're a little older."

The other mother said proudly, "Not mine. He was crawling at four months. Don't feel bad, though. His father is really smart, and he's kind of ahead of most kids. Are you encouraging him to try to crawl?"

Now, what the hell kind of question is that? Of course I'm encouraging him, but just to freak her out, I said, "No, we put him in a chicken cage at night and throw bird seeds at him."

Then I walked away.

The other type of annoying mommies are the "You really shouldn't do that" mommies. Things you hear from them will sound like this: "You really shouldn't wake up your baby in the middle of a nap—they say never to do that"; and "You really shouldn't give him juice—he won't like the taste of plain water"; and "You really shouldn't let him have a pacifier—he'll get addicted."

This is just so wrong in the mommy world, ladies. Let's put an end to it now. If you're reading this, you will now be in charge of shutting these women up in your own community and telling them that mommies cannot lecture other mommies. When they do, it makes the other mommies feel like someone's saying, "You suck. How could you not have known this? You're a bad mom."

I know it's not intentional but that's the way it makes the other mommies feel. Informing is one thing, like saying, "Oprah had a special about babies choking on certain toys." That's cool. Information, not lecturing.

So just remember that "comparison shopping" is fine, but when it comes to "competitive shopping" and "You really shouldn't do that," mommies should think twice before opening their mouths. We might fight back by saying, "Hey, your kid might know all the words to Barney the Dinosaur, but at least my kid doesn't look like Barney!"

Don't They Make Baby Vicodin?

(Teething)

One of the hardest things a mother can go through is witnessing her baby in pain. Hopefully, teething will be the only pain you'll have to witness, but it still breaks your heart. Every baby is different, so every mom should know that yours could very well not make a peep throughout the entire teething process. You're probably the same mom who didn't get any stretch marks or tear during delivery, and I hate you for that. Everybody else probably won't be so lucky.

The first tooth to come in is kind of tricky because you don't really know what to expect from your baby. My little bird cried and cried, and I did my usual checklist and still couldn't figure it out. The next day I noticed he was still in a crabby mood and drool was leaking out of his mouth like a sixteen-year-old staring at Pamela Anderson. That's when Mommy finally put two and two together and gave my son some relief with baby Tylenol.

Baby teething is one of those things that everyone and their brother will give you helpful hints for, even though you've already been told by 150 other people. So you can either skip ahead or let me be the 151st person to tell you. Here are some good tips: Really cold or partly frozen washcloths were good at times, and so were frozen bagels, cold teething rings, and my absolute favorite, baby Anbesol. Applying it with a Q-tip made it easier.

So besides endless crying and drooling, other warning signs for teething are a fever, a runny nose, and possibly diarrhea. Some babies have also been known to get a rash. My son was part of the unlucky group to experience all of these. The tricky thing for me and my husband was trying to figure out the difference between teething symptoms and actually being sick. We called our doctor so many times when he got a fever due to teething that we stopped calling even when we were unsure if he was really sick. My poor son had a raging ear infection because I tossed it off as teething. People would say "Why is your son banging his head against the wall and pulling his hair out?" I would say "Oh, he's just teething."

What an asshole I was!! That was stupid. Again, never ever feel bad about bugging your pediatrician. That's what he's there for.

Then there were those times when nothing helped. My baby was looking into my eyes, crying hard with a runny nose and a fever, and he couldn't shove his fist any deeper into his mouth. The Tylenol wasn't working, so I switched to baby Motrin and that did nothing. That's when I started yelling at my husband to do something because I didn't know what to do myself. Finally, in desperation, I called the pediatrician and asked if they made any baby Vicodin or infant codeine for teething. I just wanted my baby out of pain. Needless to say, the doc said NO and told me to hang in there with Tylenol. (I think I've been in L.A. too long.)

It's really, really hard when you're helpless. Sometimes it takes a couple of weeks for a tooth to finally come up and your baby will be wigging out the entire time. Once the tooth breaks the gum, most of the pain has subsided, and Junior no longer looks like a rabid dog. But just when you think you've made it through a couple of the hardest weeks yet, another tooth starts up. Teething was definitely the hardest thing for me in my son's first year. But as I said earlier, you might be the lucky bitch who escapes all of it.

If you're not, just do the best you can, and don't be afraid to call and bug your baby's pediatrician if you're unsure about symptoms. You pay him enough money to interrupt a good golf game.

No . . . NO!!
Don't Touch That!

(Babyproofing)

I f you have any dead relatives in ceramic vases, now is the time to put them on very high shelves. Baby-proofing is mandatory in my eyes. There are so many things that can happen to your baby, so why take a chance on being the idiot who doesn't babyproof? You can always ask your pediatrician to refer you to a store or simply look in the Yellow Pages. There are numerous places that will do the installation for you, or if you have a handy-dandy husband, he can do it and you can save some bucks!

I knew my baby blob wasn't going to slither over and open up the bar cabinet to have a few rum and cokes, so I waited until the day he finally sat up to start babyproofing. I knew that crawling and pulling himself up on things would be his next milestone, so Mommy had to get on it. Because my husband is a handy-dandy husband, I went to a store and purchased things to babyproof the house ourselves. Actually, I half forced my husband to do it because saving money anywhere gives me an excuse to go buy a pair of shoes. But my husband doesn't need to know that.

So, there I was in the babyproofing store, completely fascinated at how many things they offer. It kind of caused me to panic and feel guilty at the same time because the salespeople tried to sell me every safety device ever created. Whenever I said, "No, thanks," they made me feel like I was being careless for not buying that "special guard." I would tell them, "But I don't own any large plants to harness to the wall," and they would say, "Fine, but what if you get one and you don't have the harness and the plant falls on your baby, crushing him?" I couldn't believe their sales technique.

Unfortunately, it worked half the time. I did buy way more than I needed. When a salesperson is walking around shouting in your ear, "It's better to be safe than sorry," how can you argue with that?

Before you go to these stores, make sure you do a count of all the objects in your house—all the kitchen, bathroom, and bedroom cabinets. Anything your child can crawl on or open. They sell oven-door stoppers, stove guards, refrigerator guards, toilet guards, and MUCH, MUCH more. So make sure you go into these stores prepared, knowing exactly what to get for your house, so you don't wind up overbuying like this asshole.

Once everything is installed, you will find yourself a prisoner in your own home. Opening drawers and climbing over baby gates makes you feel like a mouse trying to figure out a maze. But within a week, you'll be a pro at it. You won't even think twice about clicking a button or pressing down on a handle to open things. It will come naturally, so tell your husband to stop cussing as he tries to get the refrigerator door open. If you got the hang of it, he will too.

The really, really fun part about babyproofing is watching guests come over and try to open anything in your house. I got such a kick out of seeing them try to use the toilet. Just to screw with them, I wouldn't say anything, and all we'd hear was them clanking around desperately trying to figure it out. Hey, if the toilet guard

kept Uncle Trent from taking a leak, then I knew my ten-month-old didn't have a great chance of getting it open.

Babyproofing is also a GREAT time to get rid of unwanted wedding gifts that you were forced to display in the event of the giver coming over. We gave most of ours away, and when Aunt Martha stopped by, looking for her gift, we'd say, "Evan broke it, I'm so sorry." It was so fun blaming him because he wasn't gonna tell on us.

So, as soon as you babyproof, gather up all of your unwanted ceramic cats or ugly frames and pack them away for a while or simply give them away. Now is your only chance to be free of those ugly vases you'd be forced to show off for years to come. Hee hee!

Anorexic Pets

(Your Neglected Animals)

If you've always been a pet owner, you know that pets can be considered members of your family. You've probably loved your pets more than you have some relatives or maybe even some siblings. When I was a young girl, I would dress mine up in some Barbie-style outfit and sometimes even put diapers on them and pretend they were my babies. Fortunately, I grew out of the Barbie-dressing-up phase but pretending they were my babies I never outgrew.

I've craved having a real baby ever since I was twenty. Still, I knew deep down inside that I had places to go, losers to sleep with, and ladders to climb, so having a baby just to have a baby wasn't in the cards for young Jenny. I changed direction and decided to get a dog. My first was a bulldog named JoJo, after my sister. I used to bring her to work with me on MTV, and she made many TV appearances on *Singled Out* (sometimes dressed up in Barbie clothes and tutus). Anyway, she was my bitch and I was hers. Unfortunately, after only two years she passed. It killed me. My baby had gone to doggy heaven.

So I scraped myself off the floor and searched for a new baby. I found another bulldog that I named Bubba, and for my girly pleasures, I got two shih tzus named Baby and Puppy. These dogs were the light of my life. I groomed them and gave them a doggy door in the wall of my house so they could have access to their grassy kingdom whenever they wanted. There were framed pictures of them around the house, and I even entered my bulldog in competitions. I WAS A DOGGY DORK, BUT I DIDN'T CARE! I would rock the shih tzus to sleep and curl them up on my pillow. I told myself I would spoil them until the end of time and nothing would ever get in the way of that.

But when I brought my real baby home from the hospital, I locked them outside for three months and basically ignored them. It was amazing to me, after all these years of spoiling the hell out of my pets and making them a priority—even over my husband at times—that I had so easily emotionally abandoned them. I didn't mean to, but it just happened. Evan was so new and perfect that I didn't want to take the chance of the dogs becoming jealous, so I waited and waited and waited to introduce them to my baby.

When I finally did make the introduction, the shih tzus were great with my son, but the bulldog was a jealous mess. He would try to push the baby out of the way with his massive head, but Mommy wasn't gonna let that fly. I was so freakin' torn over what to do because Bubba the bulldog was my beefy man sidekick. Whenever I got cheated on by a boyfriend or had a series cancelled, Bubba's wide shoulders were the ones I wanted to cry on. Fortunately, my sister offered to take him and she lived down the street, so we decided on shared custody. Bubba stayed with her and I got to see him whenever I wanted.

The two shih tzus let my son grab their tails and even crush them when he rolls over them. But I gotta tell ya, they don't get 75 percent of the attention they used to, and it breaks my heart. Sometimes I'll be getting ready for bed and say, "Oh, shit, I forgot to feed the dogs." Even the pink bows in their hair have been replaced with leaves or whatever brush they get into outside. My once-pampered princesses are now treated like regular dogs.

So, when it comes to your own flesh-and-blood off-spring, you're not going to let your furry friends be the boss of you. Your furry friends will take the backseat or, I should say, the back porch of your attention the moment you bring your baby home. Just let them know that you love them and that you'll be back—you just need some time to adjust. You'll know if you're neglecting them too much if they start to resemble Lara Flynn Boyle's figure. Just give them a big bowl of food and tons of kisses, and tell them that Mommy is still here for them.

Mommy, Can I Have Another Jar of Liquid Chicken and Poo-Poo-Colored Peas?

(Feedin' Time)

Milk, milk, and more milk! Got milk? NO!!! ENOUGH MILK!! Whether you're pumping it or scooping milk powder out of a container, you can't wait until your life is not consumed by milk. The day the doctor told me it was time to move my baby to pureed meat and veggies, I hugged him. Little did I know that milk was a whole lot easier.

Many women I met made their own liquid meat and

veggies. They would cook up the food, throw it in the blender with a little water, and then put it into ice-cube trays to freeze for later use. Hearing this would always make me feel like shit because I still wasn't very good at making peanut butter and jelly sandwiches, so I was very happy to see the endless jars of liquid meats and veggies available at the supermarket.

Starting your baby off on food can seem almost pointless at first because it will all slide down his or her chin. Babies don't get the idea of swallowing on the first try. Once they do, the food will go down pretty smoothly until you try a new veggie that's green and looks like poo. That's when we had fun capturing on film our baby gagging on peas. I don't blame him, though—the first time I tried some off of his baby spoon, I gagged too. Why baby food has to smell like a senior citizen's ass is beyond me.

I was totally freaked out by the time I moved my baby to solids. The first fifty times I put a piece of solid food in his mouth, he would choke. I always had one hand ready to bang on his back. I secretly wanted to keep him on pureed foods until he was sixteen, but then I pictured him on a first date asking a chef for liquid steak and knew that wouldn't be "cool" in front of his girlfriend.

My son did finally get the hang of eating solids, but any mom will tell you that it's a scary process to go through. Never leave your baby unattended, not even to pee or answer the phone, while he or she is eating. Also, there is a whole list of foods to avoid in that first year, like hot dogs, peanut butter, popcorn, egg whites, and honey, just to name a few. Do some "www" research to check it out.

You might notice your little munchkin not having an appetite at all one day and then being as hungry as an elephant the next. This is normal. My doctor always told me babies won't starve. When they're hungry, they'll eat, and they will always get the nutrients they need by the end of the week. At times, though, it will seem like your baby is doing his own fasting cleanse.

Once solids have safely gotten down your baby, you will start seeing "human poo" come out of him. So go ahead and give him more carrots and meat!! You'll see so many "logs" that you'll start to feel like a lumberjack in your own house! TIMBER!!!

www.ismybabydeveloping properly.com

(Researching Your Baby's On-Time Development)

When I was pregnant, I was addicted to going online each week and finding out what my little embryo was up to. Once I absorbed as much information as I could on one website, I would move on to the next, just in case the first had forgotten to mention that my baby was growing a kidney that week. Things didn't change much once my baby was born. I became addicted to finding out what milestones my son was supposed to be reaching each week. Even though I was so eager to find things out, I didn't become an extremist. I wouldn't call my doctor in a panic screaming, "EVAN HASN'T ROLLED OVER YET, AND IT SAYS RIGHT HERE ON *WWW. SUPERBABY.COM* THAT HE'S SUPPOSED TO. WHAT'S WRONG WITH HIM? SHOULD WE GET HIM HELP?"

There is absolutely no need to get crazy about milestones. If you ever do have a concern, simply ask your pediatrician at the next visit. Every baby I hung around with in my son's first year developed at its own pace and in its own way. Some babies never crawled. They went from rolling to pushing themselves up to walking. Some walked months before the rest of the pack. It didn't mean that one was slower than another. Your baby could be choosing to focus on learning to say "dog" instead of taking a few steps that month. This is the stage when competitive mommies have a ball. Like I told you before, don't let them get the best of you. Fight back.

I remember being SOOO excited when Evan hit any milestone. I wanted to throw him a party with hot four-month-old chicks in bikinis just to celebrate. Sometimes it felt like a hundred years before he finally hit some developmental mark. Rolling over was our toughest. My husband and I did just about everything to get him to do it—dancing, squeak toys, making up songs for rolling over.

Finally it got to the point that my husband and I would roll around on the living room floor, day after day, to physically show him how to do it. By the way, this was a great way to see what had been hiding under the furniture for months. The remote, bottles, socks. So there are some benefits to looking like a weirdo rolling around your living room floor.

Once my son finally rolled over, I felt like a whole new world had been introduced to him. He was more easily entertained watching things going on around him rather than staring at the ceiling. He had officially graduated from blob to sitting-up blob. I was so proud.

Then one night when I was giving Evan a bath, he looked at me and said, "Cow." I began to cry, not because he called me a cow, but because it was his first word. For months, that's all he said. *Cow, cow, cow.*

You will find yourself calling everyone you know to tell them your baby's first word. And, to be honest, no one really gives a shit. Your mom might think it's precious, but you will be the only one squeaking in delight. Don't even bother calling your single friends—they'll fake a burst appendix rather than listen to thirty minutes of "cow this" and "cow that."

Out of all the milestones, watching my son take his first steps and hearing him say "Ma Ma" were without doubt the best!!! It was amazing to me that, just a year earlier, my blob couldn't do anything. Now he was walking like Frankenstein through the living room, with his arms open, saying, "Ma Ma." All those months of changing crappy diapers and being puked on by your baby, without your blob even saying, "Hey, thanks," simply disappear. This is one of those moments that prove how well you've done as a mom. Because your baby couldn't have done it without you!

Cravings from the Dark Side

(Starting Up Old Habits)

The first thing I can tell you about becoming a new mom is that, from this day forward, you will be living in fear. The first type of fear you'll experience is for the well-being of your baby. *Is he breathing? Is he sick? Can he see? Can he hear?*

That will be followed up with, *Is he gonna fall off that slide? Is that other little boy gonna push him? Did he just swallow Windex?*

Then that will be followed by puberty concerns and teenage pressures: *Will he drink and do drugs?* And so on. What I'm trying to get across is that you will now and forever live in fear for your child.

The other type of fear is for the well-being of yourself and your husband. God forbid that anything happens to either of you. I was always kind of careless about my body, but now my little bird was depending on me, so I knew that mama bird better get healthy. That was THE reason I was finally able to give up smoking. I was so bad that, after I delivered, while still lying on the birthing table, I asked the nurse to wheel me out into the parking garage so I could smoke.

She didn't, but it had been nine months since I puffed on what I always called my best friend—my cigarette. It was always there for me. It never got mad at me, it never talked shit about me, it was ALWAYS there when I needed it. And it got me through some tough times. I had been smoking since I was thirteen, so I knew it would be tough to kick the habit. I was proud that I quit the moment I knew I was pregnant, but I just had to have a cigarette the moment the baby was born.

A few months went by, and I puffed-puffed away. I NEVER smoked near the baby. Even if I was outside, I wouldn't let the baby actually see me smoke. Then it happened. A Truth commercial, which is an anti-smoking campaign, came on TV. It showed a woman strolling her baby and leaving it in the middle of Times Square. She just walked away! People were all looking and walking toward the stroller, and inside was a baby doll holding a sign that said 15,000 moms leave their children motherless each year. That did it for me.

There was no way, no how, I was going to leave my baby any sooner than I had to. I looked at my cigarette like the enemy now, like it was trying to take me away from my baby. I loved my baby SOOO much that I couldn't even fathom not seeing him off to college. I walked out onto my porch, smoked a good-bye cigarette, and haven't touched one since. Whenever I had a craving, I would hold my son and stare at him. Looking into your own child's eyes makes you hit reality hard!! Once I cleared withdrawal, I never wanted to smoke again.

The only time I was a big drinker was in college. Like everybody else. What do you expect when it's nickel-draft night? It's almost part of the curriculum—you get drunk, kiss a few ugly frogs, puke on them, and go home. I think husbands and wives should have their special date nights here and there, and even get sauced up if they so desire. But if drugs or alcohol is ever a problem for you or for your husband, don't be afraid to do something about it. There are so many support groups out there, and there's nothing worse you can do for your baby than to do nothing at all.

So, just be safe out there when you choose your dark-side cravings. Have fun, but just know that there's a little life out there depending on YOU.

And the Winner of the Most Severe, Balding, Sweaty, Gum-Diseased Woman of the World Award Is . . . YOU!!!

(Letting Go of Pregnancy Hormones)

Just when you thought you were done with strange shit happening to your body . . . more strange shit happens to your body. Once I woke up in the middle of the night and knew that something seemed bizarre. I whipped the covers off me and noticed that I was completely soaked. I thought I had peed on myself. I lightly touched my husband and freaked because he was wet. I thought for sure that I'd peed on him too. I stood up and smelled the bed. It didn't smell like pee. I was so relieved. I knew my bladder wasn't up to par after giving birth, but if I had to start wearing Depend diapers to bed, I was going to lose it!!

I woke up my husband, who was completely freaked out too. When I tell you the bed was wet, I mean SOAKED, like someone emptied a couple of buckets on the bed. Even my hair was completely sopped. We both changed our pajamas and the sheets and went back to bed. But then a few hours later, when the baby woke us up, I pulled the blanket back and felt a giant breeze on my soaked body!! Not again!! I couldn't believe it. It was like Mother Nature was having fun with me.

This went on for a couple of months until my husband became tired of his bedtime "baths" and officially moved onto the couch until I was done extracting water from my alien body. This was the first physical sign of my body slowly letting go of my prego hormones.

The next thing to happen not only freaked me out but grossed me out. I was taking a shower and conditioning my fried fake-blond-and-still-trying-to-be-sexy-but-*so*-isn't hair when I noticed clumps sliding into the drain. I looked at my conditioner bottle and thought for sure someone must have put some Nair (hair remover) in there. I got out of the shower and ran a brush through my hair. With one stroke, the brush was filled, like I was holding a dead rabbit in my hand. I called out for my husband, which didn't help much. He stared at me like the freak of nature I was.

Just when I thought I was done with things happening to my body, I decided to go to the dentist since it had been a while because of my pregnancy. She did a cleaning and an exam, and told me that I had fourteen cavities and gum disease!!!!! Ugh! Gross. I took care of my teeth, but they say that pregnancy can really f*ck them up. I couldn't believe that either. I checked it out and read up on it and it turned out to be true.

So, if I were you, I wouldn't put off the dentist. The least you can do is have a pretty smile while you're going bald and drowning in your own sweat!

Supermom

(Deciding to Go Back to Work)

Y ou are so lucky if you're a mom who actually gets to choose whether to go back to work. Some aren't that lucky, so count your blessings. Leaving your baby can be incredibly hard. Earlier in the book, I talked about how I just wanted to lock myself in my room with my baby and sell Avon products from home. I couldn't even imagine passing him off to another caretaker and heading off to work. But as months went by, I knew I had to go make a buck, so I dug in and found enough strength to take my first job back.

I was asked to do an episode of *Less Than Perfect*. The first day I got there, I cried. I cried all week. I actually called the Home Shopping Network from the set to see if I could sell crap on TV so I didn't have to work full time anymore. They told me that I'd have to be the one to supply the crap to sell, not them. Considering that I had no crap to sell, I knew I had to keep trucking along.

I was picky about the jobs that would come my way. I didn't want to do anything that took me away from my baby or wasn't financially profitable. "You want me to go overseas and do a movie with Brad Pitt? . . . No, thanks, I'll take the local junkyard commercial that's paying pretty well so I can be home with my baby." (Okay, maybe I would have made an exception for a Brad Pitt movie.)

I don't mean to make going back to work sound miserable because there was an extremely positive thing that happened when I went back. I noticed that having a sense of self—doing something for me—felt really, really good. To know that I was actually good at something besides changing poo-poo diapers in thirty seconds or less, and having an audience laugh at my character rather than my maternity muumuu felt great. This part of me understood why some moms can't wait to go back to work. I definitely got it. I wanted the best of both worlds. But how does one get that?

Sadly, I still don't know. To this day, if I work all day and don't see my son, I wake him at night to play with him. I have to . . . I call it "The Working Mom Guilt Syndrome."

Ugh! . . . GUILT! My husband—this could very well be your husband, which is why I'm sharing this with you—didn't really have a problem in this area. Guilt from being away from their babies during the day doesn't seem to faze men much, but it BOGGLES the hell out of me.

If I'm coming home late from work and haven't seen the baby all day, you might see me driving on sidewalks and hitting a few pedestrians to get home fast. When I open the door, I leap toward the baby and make crazy gestures and noises to celebrate my arrival. I want my baby to know that mama bird flew back home to her nest as fast as she could.

My husband, on the other hand, will enjoy his ride home and maybe stop at the newsstand for some magazines. And when he walks in the door, he'll hit the fridge first, then the bathroom, and then go see the baby. THAT'S CRAZY TO ME!! Why they don't have the same parental instinct as we do really bothers me!! I used to think my husband was having a problem connecting with my son until my friends reported the same things about their husbands.

So don't fret if your husband doesn't walk in the door doing cartwheels at first. Someday soon he won't be able to resist your baby's open arms as he stands at the front door saying, "DA DA."

Meanwhile, if you're lucky enough to stay home and be the caretaker of your baby, good for you. Enjoy it while you can, and don't forget that doing something for yourself is so important—whether it's being really good at surfing the Internet or joining that class. The more fulfilled you are, the happier your home will be!

"Can I Take Your Order?" "Yes, God, I'll Take Another Baby with No Pickles and Extra Mustard This Time"

(Deciding on Baby #2)

Y ou look at your naked ass in the mirror and shout, "Wow, I can almost make out my old ass." Your body is somewhat back as you celebrate your baby's first birthday. You think back on all the memories and milestones you've gone through with your baby, and you smile. You can't believe that little old you survived childbirth and your baby's first year. It's such a huge accomplishment, and you feel honored to have earned the title *Mother*.

So then you start to consider turning your ass into a dump truck all over again.

Making the decision to have Baby #2 is different for everybody. Many people are content with one, and I say, good for them. I come from such a huge family that if there isn't a line for the bathroom, the house feels empty. I had a genetic urge to fill that line with bouncing toddlers. My husband fortunately shares the same desire. He wants more children, but he did admit that he was scared of having to go without sex for another year and a half. I told him that the next pregnancy I would be more understanding of his sexual needs. (Yeah, right, like that will ever happen.) Back in my mom's day, they banged out babies at yearly intervals. Now I think it's important to wait until you truly feel like getting pregnant again.

To tell you the truth, I knew I wanted another baby someday, but my pregnancy was so difficult that, for a year and a half, when people would ask when I was going to get pregnant again, I would say, "In, like, ten years." Then something amazing happened one day that I hope is recognized as scientific fact. A little something I like to call Pregnancy Amnesia set in.

One magical day, your body chemically forces your brain to forget about the hardships of pregnancy and childbirth. I believe with all my heart that this happens because many women wouldn't conceive if they remembered the pain precisely. I always wondered why my mother claimed that giving birth wasn't that bad, yet my father would go on and on about her painful cries. Now I know why—pregnancy amnesia!

It took me about a year and a half, and then one day, *BAM!* All I could think about was how badly I wanted another baby. All my aches and pains of delivery didn't seem so bad anymore. I was ready to have cottage cheese platters for thighs again. I was willing to blow out my vagina and cry when I went #2. I was ready to give Evan a little brother or sister.

Hell, at least now I knew what I was headed for, even though pregnancy amnesia blurred it a bit. I became the great mom I hoped I would become, and if I can share that with more little spirits, then all the better. I hope you enjoy being a mom as much as I do. I swear to you there's nothing better in life.

So, wish me luck out there, girls, as I embark on round two, and I'll be doing the same for you during your first year of MOMMYHOOD!!!! It's sweet, it's hard, it's thankless at times, but it's the best piece of heaven on earth. You'll see.

Tips for Mom

Don't get depressed about the size of your ass. Also, DO NOT BUY A NEW WARDOBE until you reach your goal size. Patience and effort will eventually get you out of those ugly oversized sweats.

Don't forget to be a wife. Even though baby puke is your new perfume and you're so tired that you want to hide in a small cave and sleep, your husband still needs some

TLC. A good solid marriage is so important when raising a family. Keep communication up during these times.

When you are searching for a good pediatrician, choose one with a great ass—it makes the visits more fun. I'm kidding. Get recommendations from your gyno and from friends who you trust, and interview doctors to find the one who matches your needs.

When traveling, invest in a DVD player to entertain your baby. If your baby is too small to be entertained, dress him up in the sports team uniform of the city you are traveling to. A two-month-old screaming on an airplane is a lot cuter if he's dressed as a mini Chicago Cub.

If you start to resemble a troll living under a bridge, get out and do something for yourself at least ONCE a week. Work out, take a class, go for a walk, or even just put on makeup. A pretty troll is at least better than an ugly one!

Take an extra outfit for your baby EVERYWHERE you go. Don't leave home without it. "Shitting up the back" can happen ANYWHERE!!!

If anybody asks if you need anything before they stop over for a visit, say, "YES! Diapers!!!" Even though you have plenty, you can always use more.

Do not routinely let your baby sleep in your bed. Your child will become an addict, and you won't be able to regain private use of the bed until your child leaves for college.

When you think you are truly about to crack and can't take it anymore, keep reminding yourself that it will get easier. I promise!! It really, really does!!!

Well, at least until they turn sixteen and they tell you to go bite yourself and take the family car out in the middle of the night with their friends and get drunk and don't come home and you're up late worrying half to death about them and then you tell them they can't go to the prom and they hate you and blame you for their lack of social skills later on in life and . . . oh . . . Sorry. That book will be called *Puberty Sucks* and will be available in about thirteen years.

Tips for Dad

(From Your Wife)

E ven though my ass is the size of Texas, please tell me I look pretty. I know I look like a hairy piece of steak fat, but it will make me smile.

When you are coming home from work or anywhere, please call home to see if I need anything from the store. It saves me a trip.

🪰

I know you are working so hard to bring home the bacon, but please know that I'm working JUST as hard. Once in a while, please let me know verbally, not through sex, that you appreciate all I'm doing at home with the baby. It will make me feel SOOOO good!

Plan a date for us somewhere, even if it's staying at the nice hotel down the street for the night. My mom will watch the baby, and then we can have our time and one good night's rest. I'm too busy to make arrangements, so please be the one in charge of handling it.

In the first few months, please try to help out with dinners as much as possible. It would mean so much to me if you walked in the front door with takeout.

If I'm changing the majority of the poopy diapers, please be the one to keep up with taking out the garbage filled with them. It's only fair.

If I feel like doing something for myself for like an hour or so on the weekend, please be cool and take the baby during this time. I just want to go on a bike ride or window shop.

🪰

I know you have the worst case of blueballs imaginable, but I still need you to hang in there. Even though my vagina is "healed," I just don't feel ready for sex. Please just cuddle with me, and when I finally feel frisky again, I'll rock your world. I promise.

Lastly, know that I love you. You are my man, and I'm so proud that our baby is going to be raised by such a good dad. We will both love you till the end of time.

About the Author

Jenny McCarthy is the former host of the enormously popular MTV dating show *Singled Out* and the *New York Times* best-selling author of *Belly Laughs: The Naked Truth About Pregnancy and Childbirth*. She lives in California with her husband and two-year-old son.

The author will donate a portion of her proceeds from this book to the Cystic Fibrosis Foundation to help find a cure and to improve the quality of life for those with the disease. For more information, go to http://www.cff.org.

To Henley,

You're almost 7 now, and I want you to know I'm your biggest cheerleader and hope my BIG mouth will make many people do everything they can to make your life the best it can be!

BIG hugs and kisses,

Jenny McCarthy